A DABHAND

1st Word plus

WORDPROCESSING ON THE ARCHIMEDES

ANNE ROONEY

DABS PRESS

Mastering 1st Word Plus

© Anne Rooney 1992
ISBN 1-870336-18-6
First Edition June 1992

Editor: Roger Amos.
Typesetting: Mark Nuttall
Cover: Mark Nuttall.
Internal Illustrations: Mark Nuttall and David Wilson

The text for this book was produced using 1st Word Plus on an A540.

Published by Dabs Press, 22 Warwick Street, Prestwich, Manchester M25 7HN. Tel: 061-773 8632.

Printed and bound in Great Britain by A.Wheaton & Co., Ltd, Exeter, Devon, a member of the BPCC Group.

Contents

Part 1

PART 2

Introduction: Using a wordprocessor

1st Word Plus is a word-processing program you can use with Acorn RISC OS computers. You can use it on a BBC A3000, an A5000 or any Archimedes computer. You might have chosen 1st Word Plus for your word-processing, or perhaps you bought the Learning Curve and found 1st Word Plus is part of the package. 1st Word Plus is also available for some other, non-Acorn computers, and if you have an Atari ST or a PC running 1st Word Plus you will be able to transfer files between the computers, with suitable file transfer software. 1st Word Plus enables you to use your computer for text processing. You can write letters, memos, leaflets, reports ... even party invitations or posters with pictures.

Why use a word-processor?

If you are used to using a typewriter, you will quickly notice the benefits of using a word-processor instead! It is easy to correct mistakes, change your text around, check your spelling, swap one word or phrase for another throughout your document, lay out your text elegantly and add page numbers or other text to the top or bottom of every page. Best of all, you can make all kinds of changes as often as you like before you even print out your work – then when you do print it, you have a perfect copy first time.

When you use a manual or electric typewriter, the letters you type appear on the page immediately as you type them. If you make any mistakes, you have to retype the page or use correcting fluid to cover them up. With a word-processor, though, nothing is printed until you are satisfied with it and instruct the computer to print your work. The text you type is stored in the computer's memory. You can save it, turn off the computer and come back to work on it another day without needing to print it out in between.

One advantage of a word-processor is obvious immediately as you type. You don't need to watch how far across the page your text has got and press the Return key to move to the start of the next line; 1st Word Plus automatically 'wraps' your text, moving it to the start of the next line whenever it reaches the line end. You can make all kinds of adjustments to the appearance of the text once you have got the words down. This leaves you free to think about the content of your document while you type.

1st Word Plus

1st Word Plus release 2 runs on any Acorn RISC OS computer in a window on the desktop. (The first version took over the computer, replacing the desktop.) You can use it with a dot-matrix printer, an HP LaserJet-compatible laser printer or a daisywheel printer. It comes with a special 'mail-merge' program called 1st Mail to help you prepare mailshots. These are batches of letters with the same basic content but with some variations. Typically, they have different names and addresses and a few other varying details. These change from one letter to another, but you can print all the letters in a batch, instructing 1st Mail to make the changes for you. The rest of this book explains how to use 1st Word Plus and how you can use 1st Word Plus in combination with other programs and products (Part 1), and how to use 1st Mail, the mail-merge program (Part 2).

Moving on...

The next chapter explains how to make copies of the 1st Word Plus discs, install the program on a hard disc and load 1st Word Plus into your computer.

1 Getting ready to use 1st Word Plus

Before you can use 1st Word Plus you need to load it into your computer's memory so that the icon appears on the icon bar. Before you do this, though, you should copy the 1st Word Plus discs, either onto floppy discs or onto the hard disc of your computer. This chapter explains how to copy the discs and load 1st Word Plus.

Copying the 1st Word Plus discs

1st Word Plus is supplied on two discs containing the following files:

Program disc:

◆   !1stChars

- ◆ !1stMail
- ◆ !1stWord+
- ◆ !System
- ◆ 1ML_data
- ◆ 1ML_docs
- ◆ 1WP_docs
- ◆ 1WP_pics

Utilities disc:

- ◆ !1stConvrt
- ◆ !1stMerge
- ◆ 1WP_Print

The licensing agreement provided with 1st Word Plus allows you to make copies of the program and utilities discs for your own use. You should do this immediately. You can then keep the originals as back-up copies. A back-up is a copy of a disc that you keep safely in case you lose or damage your working copy of the program. As long as you have a back-up copy, you will be able to re-copy the program and continue using it if anything happens to your working copy.

Although you are encouraged to make a copy of the 1st Word Plus discs for your own use on one computer, you are not allowed to make copies to give or sell to other people, or to use on several computers. If you do this, you will be infringing copyright legislation and may be prosecuted. However, if you want to run several copies – perhaps in your school or business – you can buy a site licence from Acorn. You can make your working copy of 1st Word Plus on a floppy or hard disc. The instructions that follow tell you how to make a copy on floppy disc and how to install 1st Word Plus on a hard disc. Read the section that is appropriate for your computer.

Copying 1st Word Plus onto floppy discs

To make a copy of each of the 1st Word Plus discs, you need to:

◆ format a new floppy disc

◆ copy the necessary files and directories onto it, either directly or by using an area of computer memory set aside as a RAM disc

◆ name and label the new copy.

The following instructions are divided into two sections, one for computers with a single floppy disc drive and one for computers with two floppy disc drives. Read the section that is appropriate to your computer.

Before you can make a copy, you need an empty, formatted disc. To format a disc, follow these steps.

1. Put the disc into the floppy drive of your computer and display the icon bar menu for that drive by moving the pointer over the disc drive icon and pressing the middle mouse button.

2. Move the pointer over the menu option **Format** and onto the submenu that appears. Select the **E-format** option.

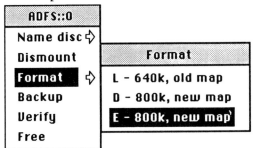

3. If you are using RISC OS 2, a window appears with a prompt asking you to confirm that you want to format the disc; click the lefthand mouse button or press the Y key on the keyboard to continue. The disc will be formatted and verified. If you are using RISC OS 3, a dialogue box will appear instead of a window. Click on Format to confirm that you want to format the disc. Whichever version of RISC OS you are using, the window or dialogue box will report the progress of the disc formatting.

4. With RISC OS 2, you will need to press the space bar or click the lefthand mouse button when formatting has finished to dismiss the window. With RISC OS 3, click on the close icon to remove the dialogue box.

Copying discs using a single floppy drive

The computer will refer to the disc you are copying from as the source disc. It will call the disc you are copying to (which you have just formatted) the destination disc. You need to write-protect the source disc, but leave the destination disc unprotected so that the computer can write to it. Follow these steps to make a copy of the Program disc.

1. Put the Program disc in the floppy drive. Display the icon bar menu for the floppy drive and select the option **Backup.**

2. A window appears with a prompt asking you to confirm that you want to make a back-up of the disc; click the lefthand mouse button or press the Y key on the keyboard to continue.

3. A message asks you to write-protect the source disc; if you haven't done this already, do it now. Put the disc into the drive and press the space bar when you are ready. The computer will copy information from the disc into its own memory. If you have a lot of free memory available, it will be able to copy all the contents of the disc. If you don't have enough, it will do the back-up in stages.

4. When the computer has copied as much of the information on the disc as it can store, a prompt will appear asking you to put the destination disc in the floppy drive. Do this and press the space bar. The computer will copy the information it has stored in its memory from the source disc onto the disc in the drive.

5. If the computer didn't have space to copy all the information in one go, it will prompt you to put the source disc back in the drive. It will copy more information from it and then ask you to put the destination disc back. This will continue for as long as it takes to copy all the information from the source disc to the destination disc. When the computer has finished the copying, you will have to press the space bar or click the mouse to dismiss the prompt window.

6. Delete the directory !System from the working copy you have just made. There is a section later in this chapter that tells you what to do with !System; you may need to copy files from it to a different disc.

7. Clearly label the copy of the disc you have made and use this as your working copy. Keep the original disc safely as a back-up copy.

Make a copy of the Utilities disc in exactly the same way, using another formatted floppy disc.

Copying discs using two floppy drives

If you have two floppy drives on your computer, making copies of discs is quicker and easier than if you have only one floppy drive. Follow these steps to copy the Program disc.

1. Put the Program disc into floppy drive :1 and a newly-formatted floppy into drive :0.

2. Display the icon bar menu for floppy drive :1 and select the option **Backup.** It is important that you use the icon bar menu of drive :1; you don't want to back-up the empty floppy onto your original Program disc or you will lose all the information on it! (As long as you have write-protected the Program disc, you won't be able to do this.)

3. A window appears with a prompt asking you to confirm that you want to make a back-up of the disc in drive :1 onto the disc in drive :0; click the lefthand mouse button or press the Y key on the keyboard to continue.

4. A message asks you to write-protect the source disc; if you haven't done this already, do it now. Put the disc into the disc drive and press the space bar when you are ready. The computer will copy information from the source disc (drive :1) onto the destination disc (drive :0). Both disc drives will operate in turn until all the information has been copied. When the copying is complete, you will have to press the space bar or click the mouse to dismiss the prompt window.

5. Delete the directory !System from the working copy you have just made. There is a section later in this chapter that tells you what to do with !System; you may need to copy files from it to a different disc.

6. Clearly label the copy of the disc you have made and use this as your working copy. Keep the original disc safely as a back-up copy.

Make a copy of the Utilities disc in exactly the same way, using another formatted floppy disc in drive :0 and putting the Utilities disc in drive :1.

Hard discs and floppy copies

If you have a hard disc, your working copy of 1st Word Plus will be on your hard disc. The next section explains how to install 1st Word Plus onto your hard disc. However, you might still want to make an extra back-up copy of 1st Word Plus on floppy discs. The licensing agreement allows you to do this.

Installing 1st Word Plus on a hard disc

If you have a computer with a hard disc, you can copy 1st Word Plus onto the hard disc. You will not then need to use the floppy discs at all, but keep them safely in case you delete or lose the copy on your hard disc.

To copy 1st Word Plus onto your hard disc, follow these steps:

1. Open a directory display for the hard disc root directory by clicking on the hard disc icon on the icon bar. You can copy 1st Word plus directly into the root directory if you like, but it is better to create a new directory specifically to hold it. To do this, move the pointer into the directory

display, then press the middle button on the
mouse to display this menu:

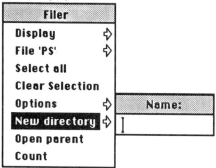

Move the pointer over the option **New directory** to
display a space for the directory name. A space you
can type in, like this, is called a writable icon. Type a
name, such as 1stWord+, for your new directory,
and then press the Return key. The name may be up
to 10 characters long, but can't include any spaces,
full stops (.), colons (:), semi-colons (;) or commas (,).

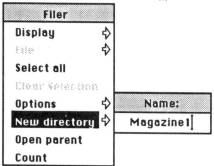

When the new directory icon appears, click on it
once with the lefthand button to open a display for
it. It will contain no icons because the new directory
is empty.

2. Before you use your 1st Word Plus discs, write-
   protect them so that you cannot accidentally
   delete the program. To do this, find the little
   black slider in one corner of the disc and move it
   (if necessary) so that it uncovers a hole in the disc.
   When the disc is protected like this, you won't be

able to add any information to it or delete anything from it, but you can read information into the computer.

3. Put the 1st Word Plus Program disc into floppy drive 0 of your computer and click with the lefthand button on the floppy disc drive icon to open a directory display showing the disc's contents:

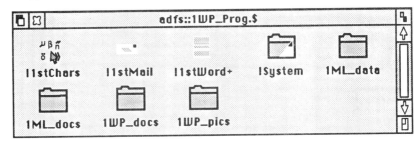

Select all the files and directories except !System. You can do this by clicking on each object in turn with the righthand mouse button; this allows you to select more than one object at once. The file and directory icons will be highlighted to show that they are selected.

4. Position the pointer over one of the highlighted icons, then press and hold down the lefthand mouse button. Now drag these icons into the display for the directory you have created to hold 1st Word Plus by moving the mouse (keeping the button pressed down) until the pointer is in the new directory display. Release the mouse button and the files and directories will be copied onto your hard disc.

You will now be able to load 1st Word Plus using the copy on the hard disc. This is described in the last section in this chapter. The next section explains what you need to do with the !System directory, if anything.

!System

Many Acorn programs need to use some shared resources. These are kept together in a directory called !System. When you first bought your computer, there will have been a !System directory on the application discs or on the hard disc with the current versions of these shared resources. The resources are called *modules* and are kept in a directory called Modules inside !System. From time to time, Acorn updates some of them, and when you buy a new Acorn program – like 1st Word Plus – it comes with a !System directory of its own that holds the most recent versions of the modules that the program needs. You should only ever have one !System directory. When you buy a program, you should copy the modules from the !System supplied on the Program disc into the Modules directory in your own !System directory (if they are more recent than those you already have).

Whether or not you need to copy any of the modules from the !System directory depends on which version of RISC OS you have on your computer.

RISC OS 3

If you are running RISC OS 3, don't copy any part of the !System directory onto your hard disc or onto your working disc or !System disc. The versions that you already have will be more recent than those on the 1st Word Plus disc and you will encounter problems if you try to use those supplied with 1st Word Plus Release 2. (If another version of 1st Word Plus is released, this may have new versions of the modules on it; this advice relates only to Release 2.)

RISC OS 2

If you are running RISC OS 2, you should copy the modules from the 1st Word Plus program disc that are more recent than those you already have into your own Modules directory.

If you have a floppy disc system, follow these instructions:

1. Find the disc on which you keep !System. This is likely to be Apps1 that came with your computer. Open a directory display for the disc and then hold down Shift and double-click on !System to open the directory. The directory display will show the contents of !System: !Boot, !Run, !Sprites and the directory called Modules. Double-click on Modules to open a directory display for it.

2. Now open a directory display for !System on the 1st Word Plus Program disc and for its Modules directory. This has fewer files in it than your existing Modules directory, so you can't just overwrite the old one with the new one.

3 You now need to set the Copy options ready to copy files from the 1st Word Plus Modules directory into your own directory. Press F12 to go to the command line at the bottom of the screen, then type:

```
set copy$options F N P
```

and press the Return key twice. This sets the Copy options to:

◆ overwrite any existing files and directories of the same name

◆ only copy newer versions of existing files and directories

19

◆ prompt you to replace the disc as necessary during copying. If you have two disc drives, you don't need to include the P as you won't need to switch discs.

4. You can now copy the modules from the 1st Word Plus disc into the Modules directory on your !System disc. Select them all and drag them into the directory display for your own Modules directory. If you have a single floppy disc system, the computer will prompt you to switch between the discs as necessary. Close the directory directory when copying is complete.

If you have a hard disc on your computer, follow these instructions.

1. Open a directory viewer for !System. !System will probably be in the root directory or in the directory Apps1. Now hold down Shift and double-click on !System to open the directory. The directory viewer will show the contents of !System: !Boot, !Run, !Sprites and the directory called Modules. Double-click on Modules to open a directory display for it.

2. Now open a directory display for !System on the 1st Word Plus Program disc, and for its Modules directory. This has fewer files in it than your existing Modules directory, so you can't just overwrite the old one with the new one.

3. You now need to set the Copy options ready to copy files from the 1st Word Plus Modules directory into your own directory. Press F12 to go to the command line at the bottom of the screen, then type:

```
set copy$options F N
```

and press the Return key twice. This sets the copy options to:

◆ overwrite any existing files and directories of the same name

◆ only copy newer versions of existing files and directories.

4. You can now copy the modules from the 1st Word Plus disc into the Modules directory on your !System disc. Select them all and drag them into the directory viewer for your own Modules directory. Close the directory displays when copying is complete.

Once you have copied any modules you need, you can load 1st Word Plus. Remember, if you are using RISC OS 3, you don't need to copy any modules at all.

Loading 1st Word Plus

Once you have made a copy of 1st Word Plus, you are ready to begin using the program. If you are using floppy discs, always work from your copies, keeping the original program discs you bought as back-ups.

Open a directory display for the directory containing 1st Word Plus. If you are using floppy discs, you will need to put your working copy of the Program disc into the disc drive. Double-click with the lefthand mouse button on the 1st Word Plus icon. After a few moments, the 1st Word Plus icon will appear on the icon bar at the bottom of the screen.

You can now open a new 1st Word Plus document by clicking once on this icon with the lefthand mouse button. The new document window looks like this:

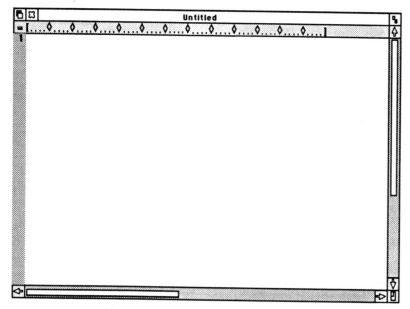

Turn to the next chapter to find out about the document window!

Moving on...

The next chapter describes the features of the two 1st Word Plus windows and takes a quick look at the 1st Word Plus menus.

2 Looking at 1st Word Plus

1st Word Plus uses two windows. The window that appears on screen when you click on the 1st Word Plus icon on the icon bar is the document window. This is the window in which your typing will appear, and you will do all your text editing and layout. There is also another window, called the keypad window, that offers some other functions and that you will need to use less often. This chapter looks at the two windows and introduces the 1st Word Plus menus.

The document window

The 1st Word Plus document window shares many features with other RISC OS windows:

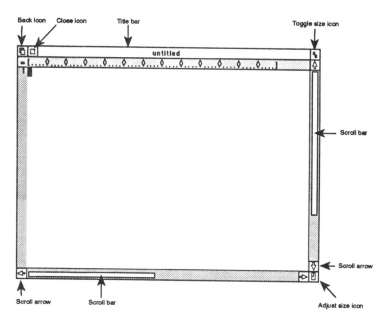

The title bar shows the name of your document. If it is a new document, it will have 'Untitled' as its name. If you have made any changes to the document since opening it, there will be a star (*) at the end of the name. This lets you see at a glance whether you need to save the document if you are going to stop working or turn off the computer.

Click on the close icon to close down the document. If you have made any changes since opening or saving it, a warning dialogue box will give you the chance to save your work before you close down the file. If you don't save your work, your changes will be lost. Saving files is described in chapter 14: Saving your work.

The back icon lets you send this window to the back of a stack of windows on the screen. If you have several windows open at once, you can use this to help you reorder them and reveal the one you want to work on. Sending a window to the back doesn't close the file.

The scroll bars along the bottom and the righthand edge of the window show how much of the document is visible on screen. If the document is too long (or too wide) for you to see all of it at once, you can drag the scroll bar, or click in the dark area outside the scroll bar to make another part of the document visible. If you want to move the document through the window in small steps, you can click one of the arrows at either end of the scroll bars.

The 1st Word Plus window also has some other features of its own. The bar along the top, beneath the title bar, is the ruler. This shows the width of the document and the positions of any tab stops. By default, a new 1st Word Plus document is 65 characters wide, with tab stops at every fifth character position. The small icon to the left of the ruler allows you to modify the ruler. You can double-click on this to display a dialogue box that allows you to make settings to adjust the current ruler. Don't worry about this for now, we'll come to ruler settings later!

Beneath the ruler icon, in the lefthand margin, is a figure 1. This is a page number. As you type and your document grows longer, it will spread onto more pages, and other page numbers will appear in the margin. You can also add page breaks wherever you like and these, too, will generate new page numbers.

In the document window, initially at the start of the first line, is a flashing black block. This is the cursor. It shows the position at which text you type will appear. As you type, the cursor moves across the screen. When you have some text in the document, you can move the cursor around. You can move the cursor by putting the pointer where you want the cursor and clicking the lefthand mouse button. The cursor moves to the new position immediately. You can also move the cursor using the scroll bar and the cursor keys. When you use the scroll bar to move through the document, the cursor always appears at the top lefthand corner of the window when the window is redrawn. The cursor keys are described in the next chapter.

1st Word Plus menus

The 1st Word Plus main menu is available from the document window. Press the menu (middle) button on the mouse to display the menu:

```
┌─────────────────────┐
│    1stWord+         │
├─────────────────────┤
│  Save          ⇨   │
│  Edit          ⇨   │
│  Select        ⇨   │
│  Layout        ⇨   │
│  Style         ⇨   │
│  Spelling      ⇨   │
│  Graphics      ⇨   │
│  Help          ⇨   │
└─────────────────────┘
```

A quick look down the list of menu tasks shows the sort of operations you can perform in 1st Word Plus – saving files, editing text, selecting text ready for editing and layout operations, setting layout and style options, checking spelling, adding graphics – and getting help if you have a problem.

Most tasks are fairly sensibly placed in the menu structure, but there are a few surprises. Reformatting a document, for example, comes in the Style menu, though really it's a layout task.

To display the sub-menu for each type of operation, move the pointer over the menu option and to the right, following the arrow. As in other RISC OS menus, a menu option followed by three dots leads to a dialogue box when you select it. Other options have an immediate effect when you click on them.

We'll return to the document window in the next chapter to begin work, but now let's take a quick look at the keypad window.

The keypad window

Move the pointer over the 1st Word Plus icon on the icon bar and press the middle button on the mouse to display this menu:

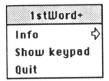

Info displays the name and version number of the program, and Quit closes down 1st Word Plus and removes its icon from the icon bar. The other option, Show keypad, is the one you need to use now. Click on this, and the keypad appears on the screen:

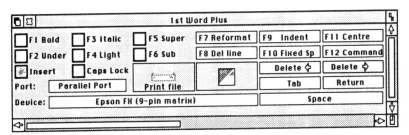

(Except on A5000 and A540 machines, if you have a multi-sync monitor and are using mode 27 or mode 28, the keypad may slightly overlap the edges of the screen so that you won't be able to see both the back icon and the toggle size icon fully at the same time. This doesn't matter, but you can switch to mode 20 if it bothers you.)

Many of the icons on this window offer the same functions as keys on the keyboard. The function keys are represented, and the tasks of the Insert, Caps Lock, Delete or Backspace, Copy (delete current character), Tab, Return and Spacebar keys are duplicated on the keypad window. You may find you never use these; it is troublesome to display the keypad window over your text to use tasks that are available from the keyboard and, in many cases, also the menus. However, you will need to use the keypad to:

◆   change the port the printer is connected to

◆   print a file

◆   load a supplementary dictionary

◆   load a printer driver.

All these operations are described later. For now, you can click on the Port icon to see how the options cycle from Parallel Port, through Serial Port to Network Port. If you click on the Print file, Dictionary or Device icons, a dialogue box will tell you briefly how to use these. Click on OK to remove the dialogue box.

Moving on...

In the next chapter you can begin typing text and we will look at some of the differences between typing on a typewriter and with a word-processor.

3   Typing text

If you have never used a word-processor before, you will find it much easier than typing with a typewriter. There are some special keys on the keyboard that you don't find on a typewriter keyboard, and there are some differences in the way you use the keys.

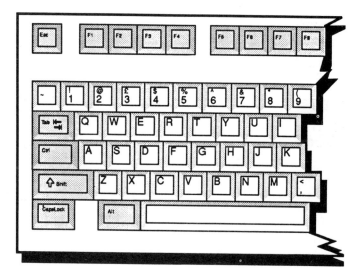

Looking at the keyboard

The keyboard is illustrated above.

Most of the keys are the same as those you would expect to find on a typewriter. However, there are some extra keys, and some variation. The keys along the top, which will be red if you have an A3000 or A300 series machine, or dark grey if you have an A400 series, A400/1 series, A5000, R260 or A540, are the *function keys*. As the name suggests, they each have a special function assigned to them. This varies between applications; in 1st Word Plus, their functions are:

F1 Bold text

F2 Underlined text

F3 Italic text

F4 Light text

F5 Superscript text

F6 Subscript text

F7 Reformat paragraph

F8 Delete line

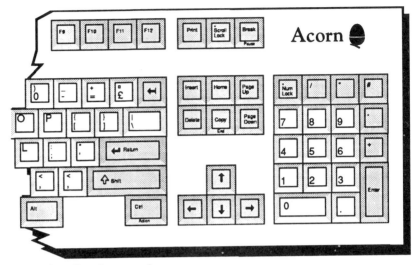

F9 Indent line/paragraph

F10 Add a fixed space

F11 Centre text in the line

F12 Go to the command line

With the exception of F8, F10 and F12, these functions are also available from the menus and we will look at how to use them later.

F8 deletes the line in which the cursor is positioned. F10 adds a space which won't be broken over a line break, and F12 allows you to leave the desktop and type at the command line. To return to the desktop, press the Return key.

To the left of the function keys is the Escape key. You can press this to abort printing a 1st Word Plus document.

The typewriter keys are much the same as those you would find on a typewriter. The main differences are the presence of the Control (Ctrl) and Alt keys, and that there is a Caps Lock key instead of a Shift Lock.

The Control key is used with some of the function keys to give extra functions. For example, if you press Control and F2 at the same time, a dialogue box appears for you to type some text you want to search for in your document:

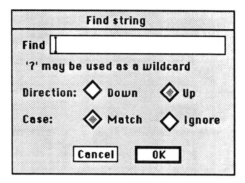

In this book, an instruction to press two keys together like this is shown in the form Ctrl-F2. In the 1st Word Plus menus, the symbol ^ is used to denote the Control key, so Ctrl-F2 appears as ^F2.

If you press down the Caps Lock key so that the light on the key is illuminated, all the letter keys will be locked so that they give capitals when you press them. This differs from a Shift Lock key in that it affects only the letters; if you press the 7 key, a 7 will appear in your document, not &. There is no Shift Lock key on the Archimedes series, A5000 and BBC A3000 computers.

The numeric keypad on the extreme right can be locked to numbers or used in some applications to access different functions. In 1st Word Plus, you can use it to type numbers when the Num Lock light is on. The Enter key has the same effect as the Return key.

The cursor keys to the left of the numeric keypad let you move the cursor about within the text. You can move the cursor up, down, left or right by a single character or more. You can also use the left and right cursor keys with Shift to move the cursor to the start of the next word or end of the last word, and with Control to move to the start or end of the line. You can use the up and down cursor keys with Shift to move up or down a screenful of text, or with Control to move to the start or end of the document.

The block of keys above the cursor keys have these functions in 1st Word Plus:

Insert – switches between overstrike and insert mode. This is described below.

Delete – deletes the character to the left of the cursor and moves the cursor back a space.

Home – has no effect in 1st Word Plus

Copy – deletes the character at the cursor position. Used with Shift, Copy deletes from the cursor position to the start of the next word. Used with Control, Copy deletes from the cursor position to the end of the line.

Page up – moves the cursor up a screenful of text.

Page down – moves the cursor down a screenful of text.

The keys above this block are not used in 1st Word Plus, but Break has its usual function, so don't experiment with this one without saving your work first! (Break on its own has no effect; Shift-Break resets the machine without using your boot file; Ctrl-Break resets the machine using your boot file if you have one.)

Using Return

When you use a typewriter, you need to press the Carriage Return key each time you want to start a new line. You use it not only to start a new paragraph, but when you have reached the end of the line you are typing and are about to run out of paper.

With a word-processor, you don't need to use Return except when you want to start a new paragraph or add a fixed line break. You can carry on typing after the cursor has reached the righthand edge of the ruler (shown at the top of the window), and the cursor will automatically jump to the start of the next line, taking the first part of the word with it if you are in the middle of a word. This feature is called *text wrap-round*. So to type the following text, you need to press Return only twice, shown by <Return>:

```
BOOKING A HOLIDAY<Return>
```

```
When you want to book a holiday, it
is usual to go to the travel agent
and collect a pile of brochures. You
can then look through the brochures
at home and choose the holiday you
want. You can book the holiday
directly with the company that
publishes the brochure, or you can go
back to the travel agent.<Return>
```

When you need a line break, press Return. So to type an address, you would press Return at the end of each line:

```
15 Dewberry Gardens<Return>
```

```
Camberley<Return>
```

```
Surrey<Return>
```

```
GU13 6RF<Return>
```

1st Word Plus counts all the text between Returns as a paragraph, even if it is only one line. Text within a paragraph can be reformatted using F7, but if you put Returns at the end of each line, F7 will only reformat one line.

Overstrike and insert

You have already met the Insert key briefly. This allows you to switch between insert mode and overstrike mode. In insert mode, you can move the cursor onto some existing text and begin typing and the text will move forward to make space for the new text you type. In overstrike mode, if you type over existing text the new text will replace the old text. So if you have text like this:

```
If you want to book a holiday, it is
usual
```

and you position the cursor after 'a' and type 'foreign' in insert mode, the line will read:

```
If you want to book a foreign
holiday, it is usual
```

But if you type in overstrike mode, the line will read:

```
If you want to book a foreign, it is
usual
```

When you first start up 1st Word Plus, it comes on in insert mode. This is generally the most useful.

To switch between insert and overstrike mode, press the Insert key. This is a 'toggle' switch – it toggles between the two modes.

L and one, O and zero

When you use a typewriter, you can often get away with using lower-case L (l) in place of one (1). A few typewriters don't have a one key at all, forcing you to use lower-case L. Similarly, you can often use capital O in place of zero (0). You shouldn't do this when you use a word-processor. You can't use l/1 and O/0 interchangeably if you use the word-processor to write computer programs because the computer won't recognise what you have done and your program will generate error messages. Even if you are just writing text, you shouldn't do it. If you want to search for, say, the date 1966 and you have sometimes used one (1966) and sometimes used lower-case L (l966), the search routine will only find the instances where you have used the character that matches what you typed in the Find dialogue box. If you type l(L)966 in the Find dialogue box, 1(one)966 won't be found in the text; if you type 1(one)966 in the Find dialogue box, l(L)966 won't be found in the text. In most typefaces, O and 0 are very different anyway, and 1 and l are often quite distinct: your work will look messy if you use the wrong character.

Typing numbers

You can type numbers in a 1st Word Plus document either by using the number keys in the top row of the typewriter keys, or using the numeric keypad with Num Lock set on. It makes no difference which you use.

Deleting letters

Every now and then, you will make a mistake while you are typing. If you spot this immediately, and it is only a letter or two, there are three keys you can use to delete the letters.

The Backspace key (to the right of the pound-sign) deletes the key to the left of the cursor and moves the cursor back a space. Any text to the right of the cursor moves back one space.

The Delete key in the block above the cursor keys has the same action as the Backspace key.

The Copy key, next to the Delete key, deletes the character directly at the cursor position. Any text to the right of the cursor moves back one space.

So with the cursor on 'y' in the following line:

```
If you want to book a holiday, it is
usual
```

pressing the Backspace or Delete key three times would give:

```
If you want to book a holy, it is
usual
```

pressing the Copy key three times would give:

```
If you want to book a holidait is
usual
```

If you want to delete a whole word, use Shift-Copy. If you want to delete to the end of the line, use Ctrl-Copy. If you want to delete more text than this, use the Delete option from the menu or function keys. This is described in chapter 6: Editing text.

Keyboard shortcuts

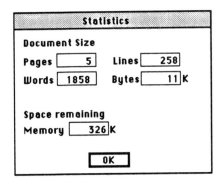

To start with, you will probably use the menus to call up all the editing and layout options available in 1st Word Plus. You can also get many of them from key presses, though, and once you get used to 1st Word Plus you will find this is a quicker way to work. There is a full list of keyboard shortcuts in Appendix 3. An example you can try immediately is Ctrl-Z. This displays a dialogue box showing statistics about your document:

You can also display this using the option Statistics in the Edit menu.

Special characters

Sometimes, particularly if you ever type text in a language other than English, you may need to use some characters which are not on the standard typewriter keyboard. Examples are: ‡, È, Ó, Ù, ≈. You can include characters such as these in your document using !1stChars. When you click on !1stChars, this window appears showing the full character set available:

When you want to include a special character, click on it in the !1stChars window and it will appear at the cursor position in your 1st Word Plus document.

You can also include a !1stChars character by positioning the cursor in the 1st Word Plus document and moving the pointer over the character you want in the !Chars window, then pressing the Shift key. This method allows you to include special characters in the text you type in a dialogue box – clicking in another window would make the dialogue box disappear. You can use this method when you want to search for text containing special characters, for example, and need to show characters from !Chars in the Find dialogue box.

Moving on...

The next chapter explains how to use special styling effects such as bold and italic to enhance your text.

4　Styling text

1st Word Plus offers you several styling options to create special effects in your text. You can use bold text, italic text, underlining, light text and super- or sub-scripted text. Often, you will want to apply these effects to text you have already typed, in which case you will need to select the text you want to change. You can also turn on one of these effects to be used for text you are about to type, and then turn it off again when you have finished with it and want to type normal text. This chapter explains how to select text and use the styling options.

Selecting text

When you want to style text you have already typed, or perform some editing tasks with text, you need to select the text you want to alter. To select text, move the cursor to the start of the piece of text you want to use, then hold down the lefthand mouse button and drag to the end of the text. The text is highlighted as white against a black background to show that it is selected. It looks like this:

To select text, move the cursor to the start of the piece of text you want to use then hold down the lefthand mouse button and drag to the end of the text. **The text is highlighted as white against a black background to show that it is selected.** It looks like this

If you want to select more text than you can see on the screen at one time, you can use a different procedure. Position the cursor over the first character you want included in the selection and use **Start** from the Select menu, or press Ctrl-S. Now position the cursor on the character *after* the last character you want included in the selection and use **End** from the Select menu, or press Ctrl-E. All the text between the two positions will be highlighted.

If you select text by dragging across it, you can only select from top to bottom, start to finish. If you are using the **Start** and **End** options, though, you can select the end first if you want to. You can also use these two to move the end or starting position of a text selection. For example, to deselect from the end of the word 'background' in the selection shown above, put the cursor on the 'd' of 'background' and use **End** or Ctrl-E to change the selection. If you move the end or start positions so that they come in the wrong order (the end before the start) you will end up with no selected text.

Once you have selected text, you can change its style; delete, copy or move it; change its case; or save it on its own as a new document. If you decide not to do anything with the text you have selected, you can clear (deselect) it. To clear selected text, you can use any of these methods:

◆ Select some different text

◆ Press and hold down the lefthand mouse button for a second or so, until the highlighting on the selected text disappears

◆ Use **Clear** from the Select menu

◆ Press Ctrl-K.

If you have a very long document, you might sometimes have some text selected in an area of the document not currently on screen. If you want to find the selected text, you can move to the beginning or end of the selection using **Find start** or **Find end** from the Select menu, or the key presses Ctrl-T to move to the start or Ctrl-B to move to the end of the selection.

Using text styles

You can give a style to a text selection by using one of the options in the style sub-menu. All the selected text will be affected by the styling option you choose. The styles are described below. There are also function key alternatives to the menu options, which are shown beside the styles in the menu and given below in the descriptions of text styles.

If you select up to the end of the text you have typed, you might find when you continue to type that the special effect you have chosen also affects the new text you type. This is because 1st Word Plus inserts an invisible marker to tell it where a special effect ends. If this is at the end of the document, the marker can be 'pushed' along in front of the cursor as you type, always remaining at the end of the document. If this happens, use the menu option or function key for the effect you have chosen to turn it off again for your new text.

43

Sometimes, you will know that you want the text you are about to type to be bold, italic, or whatever. You don't then need to type it and then select it and change the style. You can turn on the special effect you want before you type the text. To do this, choose the effect you want from the Select menu or using the function keys, then type the text you want to use that effect. When you have finished typing it, use the same menu option or function key to turn the effect off again.

The rest of this chapter describes the various text styles available and how to use them.

Bold

Bold text looks like this.

To make text bold, use Bold from the Style menu or press F1. When you make some text bold, you will see why normal text in 1st Word Plus is displayed as grey and not black: black is used to distinguish bold text. Use bold text for emphasis.

Italic

Italic text looks like this.

To make text italic, use **Italic** from the Style menu or press F3. Sometimes, it might look as if part of the last italic letter has been cropped off. This is a fault of the screen display, and won't affect how your text is printed. Use italic text for emphasis and for titles of books and articles.

Underline

<u>Underlined text looks like this.</u>

To underline text, use Underline from the Style menu or press F2.

Light

Light text looks like this.

To make text light, use **Light** from the Style menu or press **F4**. Not all printers can reproduce light text, and this is also the only special effect that won't be imported into Acorn Desktop Publisher or Impression if you use your document in one of these packages later. (By default, Impression loads light text as text using Corpus font.) Light text has a special function: it is used in the 1stMail program, described later in this book.

Super- and subscript

The following text is ^{superscript} and this is $_{subscript}$

Superscript is small text that appears in the top half of the line. Subscript is small text that appears in the bottom half of the line. You can use superscript to show powers in mathematics, eg $2^4 = 16$. 1st Word Plus uses superscript to show footnotes like this.[1] You can use subscript in chemical formulae, eg H_2O is water. If you import your document into a desktop publishing package or print it out using a suitable printer, subscript text will appear in its proper place, below the level of the line, and superscript will appear above the line. You might notice some problems with superscript italic text: 8 and 6 look alike, and 9 and 5 look alike. They are generally all right when printed, though this depends on your printer.

Moving on...

The next chapter explains how to control the layout of your document on the page, including effects such as centred text, flush left and right margins, and using tabs and indents.

5 Text layout

1st Word Plus allows you to control how your text is arranged on the page. You can have your text justified or ragged at the righthand margin, centred between the margins, aligned with the right margin, indented from the left, or tabulated. This chapter explains how to achieve all of these.

Text justification

Usually, text in books is left- and right-justified. This means that it is flush with the left and right margins. Using 1st Word Plus, you can have your text justified:

My father's family name being Pirrip, and my christian name Philip, my infant tongue could make of both names nothing longer or more explicit than Pip. So I called myself Pip, and came to be called Pip.

or left-aligned but 'ragged' at the right margin:

My father's family name being Pirrip, and my christian name
Philip, my infant tongue could make of both names nothing longer
or more explicit than Pip. So I called myself Pip, and came to be
called Pip.

or right-aligned and ragged at the left margin:

My father's family name being Pirrip, and my christian name
Philip, my infant tongue could make of both names nothing
longer or more explicit than Pip. So I called myself Pip,
and came to be called Pip.

Justified text

When you first type in a new 1st Word Plus
document, the text will be left-aligned. If you want
it justified, you will need to change the setting on
the ruler dialogue box. Rulers are described later in
this chapter. For now, we will just look at the Justify
setting on this dialogue box and ignore the rest of it.

If you want your whole document to have justified
text, move the cursor to the top of the text and use
Add ruler in the Layout menu, or press Ctrl-A. This
adds a new ruler; we'll look at rulers later. The
dialogue box that appears allows you to make
settings for the new ruler:

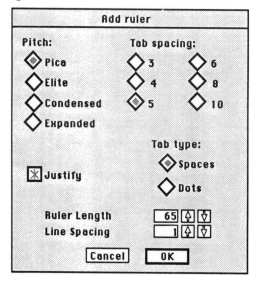

Click to place a star in the option icon beside **Justify,** and then click on OK. This will not immediately affect the appearance of the text on screen. You need to reformat paragraphs using the new ruler to see the justified text. To reformat the paragraph in which the cursor is positioned, use **Reformat Paragraph** in the Style menu, or press F7. There are two other options in the Reformat sub-menu: reformat **Between rulers,** and reformat **Whole document.** If you want to change your whole document to justified text, use the last option. If you have several different rulers set in your document, you might want to reformat only the text using the current ruler. Wherever the cursor is between the rulers, **Reformat Between rulers** will reformat all the text from the last ruler to the next ruler, including paragraphs that come before the cursor position. **Reformat Whole document** will reformat all the text in the document using the rulers in place throughout. It doesn't matter where the cursor is in the document when you choose this option – even text before the cursor position will be reformatted.

A word of warning: if you reformat a paragraph that ends with a space or with a hyphen (-), the Return immediately following it will be lost. If you had a blank line between paragraphs, the blank line after the paragraph will be lost. If you didn't have a blank line, this paragraph will be run on with the next.

When you display the ruler dialogue box, the settings shown will be those for the current ruler. So if you are using justified text and want to include some unjustified text, display the ruler dialogue box and click to remove the star from the Justify option icon.

When you type justified text, or reformat text with a ruler set to Justify, 1st Word Plus adds 'padding' or 'soft' spaces between words to fit the line between the margins. Some words will then appear to have two spaces separating them from the next word. However, if you put the cursor on the first character of the next word and press the Backspace or Delete key once, both spaces are deleted at once. This is because the padding space isn't a 'real' space – it is something 1st Word Plus identifies differently, so that it can be used or removed as necessary to fit the line to the margins.

If you have two words that you want to keep together with a single space, you can use a fixed space between them. To add a fixed space, delete the ordinary space between the two words and then press F10 with the cursor on the first letter of the second word. 1st Word Plus won't then add padding spaces between the words when fitting text to the line, and won't divide the words over a line break.

Any text you type after adding a new ruler will use the new settings, so if you change to or from justified text in the middle of a paragraph, part of the paragraph will be justified and part will be unjustified. However, when you reformat the paragraph or document, the first ruler set for a paragraph will be used to determine the layout and justification for the whole paragraph.

Right-aligned text

1st Word Plus will let you align text with the righthand margin, but as it is relatively unlikely that you will want all your text aligned in this way, you can only right-align one line at a time. To align a line of text with the right margin, place the cursor anywhere in the line and use **Right** from the Style menu, or press Ctrl-F11. The end of the line will be moved to the right margin:

This is left-aligned text which extends between the left and right margins.

This is right aligned text.

If you want to change a whole paragraph to right-aligned text, you need to change each line in turn. If you later reformat the paragraph, the first line will retain its alignment, but the other lines will be left-aligned, indented so that they start directly beneath the start of the first line. You will then have indented text with only the first line right-aligned.

If you have right-aligned text and you want to return it to left-aligned, put the cursor on the first character in the line and press the Backspace or Delete key once. All the spaces before the first character will be deleted by this one key press, and the text will move back to the left margin.

Centred text

Centred text is positioned centrally between the two text margins; this may not be centrally on the page, depending on the ruler you use in 1st Word Plus and the print margins you set for your printer.

To centre a line of text, put the cursor anywhere in the line and use **Centre** from the Style menu or press F11. Like right-alignment, centring operates on a single line at a time; you can't centre a whole paragraph at once.

Similarly, if you reformat a paragraph in which you have centred all the lines, the first line will remain centred and the others will be indented to align with its start. To return a centred line to left-alignment, put the cursor on the first character in the line and press the Backspace or Delete key once.

Working with rulers

As we saw earlier, 1st Word Plus uses a system of rulers to control some aspects of the page layout. You can use as many rulers as you like in a document. A ruler controls:

the pitch – this is the density of the characters and how they are spaced; it is described below.

tab spacing – the number of character positions between tab stops.

tab type – how tabs are separated when you use them, either by inserting spaces or inserting dots between text at different tab positions.

justification – whether text is justified or not.

ruler length – how many characters per line are allowed.

line spacing – how much space is left between lines of text.

All these settings are controlled from the dialogue box shown earlier that is displayed by **Add ruler** in the Layout menu or by pressing Ctrl-A. As well as adding a new ruler, you can alter an existing ruler. This uses the same dialogue box, though it has a different title. To modify an existing ruler, double-click on the ruler icon beside the ruler. The ruler icon looks like this:

ш

The dialogue box shown on page 48 appears. The modification will affect the full extent of the text covered by the ruler, but changes won't appear in the text unless you reformat it.

Pitch

The pitch controls how many characters will appear per inch. The appearance of the text on screen won't change, but when you print out the text, using a suitable printer and printer driver, the characters will be compressed or expanded to the pitch you have chosen. The pitch settings correspond to these type densities:

Pica: 10 characters per inch

Elite: 12 characters per inch

Condensed: $17\,^{1}\!/_{4}$ characters per inch

Expanded: 6 characters per inch

The pitch you choose won't affect the appearance of the text on screen, but if you use a suitable printer and printer driver to print out your text, it will affect the appearance of the printed text. On screen, the only difference you will see is the altered ruler length...

Ruler length

The ruler length is given a default value depending on the pitch you choose. The defaults all give a ruler width of 6.5 inches, using these numbers of characters:

Pica: 65 characters

Elite: 78 characters

Condensed: 112 characters

Expanded: 39 characters.

You can alter the value to any figure you like to a maximum of 160, either using the arrow icons to increment or reduce the value shown by one at a time, or by typing a value in the writable icon. The ruler length shows how many characters will fit on a line before word-wrap forces them onto the next line. You should set it to a value that is suitable for your printer and the paper you intend to use. For example, if you want to use A4 paper, any of the default values will give a line that fits across the page with sensible printer margins. If you want to use wider or narrower paper, you will have to adjust the ruler length accordingly.

Tabs

Tab stops in a 1st Word Plus document are the same as tabs on a typewriter. When you press the Tab key, the cursor will jump to the next tab position. It will insert spaces or dots between its original position and the tab position.

```
This text is tabbed                        with          spaces
This text is tabbed. . . . . . . . . . . . . . . . . . .with . . . . . . .dots
```

You should use tabs when you want to arrange text in a table. It is a quick way of lining up the columns without having to type spaces between them.

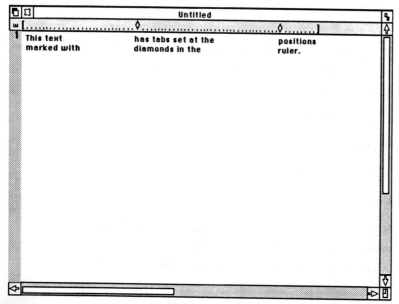

The ruler length and tab positions are shown along the top of the 1st Word Plus document window as long as **Show ruler** in the Layout menu is enabled. When the tabs are separated by spaces and are set at an interval of five spaces, the ruler looks like this:

When the tabs are set to dots, the ruler looks like this:

Each diamond marks a tab position.

You can also set tab positions at irregular intervals. To add a tab stop, click on the ruler at the position you want it to appear. To remove an existing tab stop, click on it in the ruler. These changes will not affect existing text, though they will be used for any new tabbed text you type within the ruler's extent.

By default, the tabs set in a ruler left-align text at the tab position. However, you can also set decimal tabs. A decimal tab aligns the columns so that a full stop (used as a decimal point) always comes at the tab position. It is most suitable when you are building up a table of numbers. If you don't include a full stop at all, the end of the word or number will come at the tab position, giving the same effect as a right-aligned tab. The table below shows left tabs used for the text and decimal tabs for the figures.

Furniture	prices	£.p
Table	small	120.00
Table	large	230.00
Chair	dining	78.00
3 piece suite		1200.00

To add a decimal tab, or change an existing tab to a decimal tab, double-click at the position on the ruler where you want the tab to appear. A decimal tab is marked by a hash (#) symbol on the ruler.

To use decimal tabs, you need to create the decimal tab, then press Tab to move the cursor to the tab position before you type the text. If the text includes a decimal point (full stop) or space, that will appear at the tab position. Otherwise the text will be right-aligned at the tab position. When you are using left tabs, you can insert a tab before existing text and it will move to the tab position. If you try to do this with a decimal tab, or change a tab from left to decimal when there is already text at the tab position, the start of the text will fall at the tab position as if it were a left tab.

If you use tabs in text that you then reformat with justification set on, padding spaces may be added between the tab positions and result in tabbed text not aligning with the tabs after all. Look out for this and delete any extra spaces as necessary. (If you still want the text to reach the end of the line you will need to add the spaces you have deleted back in elsewhere in the line.)

Line Spacing

By default, 1st Word Plus uses single line spacing. You can increase the line spacing to double spacing or more using the writable icon or arrow icons on the Modify ruler dialogue box. If you choose double spacing, an extra blank line will be added between all the lines of text as you type new text or when you reformat existing text. If you choose three-line spacing, an extra two blank lines will be added, and so on.

Setting margins

When you set the length of the ruler, it always begins at the lefthand margin of the page. If you want a ruler that begins some way in from the left margin, you can move the start by dragging the open bracket at the lefthand edge of the ruler to the position you want the ruler to start at. You can move the righthand limit of the ruler in the same way. Moving the start of the ruler is useful if you want to include a section of indented text comprising more than one or two paragraphs.

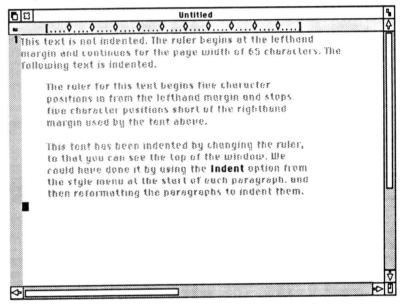

You can use the **Indent** option to do this, but then you have to indent each paragraph explicitly. Indenting text is described below. If you use a ruler with an altered left margin, everything you type or reformat within the extent of the ruler will use its left margin.

At any time you can find out the extent of the current ruler by positioning the pointer over the ruler icon at the top of the document window and pressing and holding down the lefthand mouse button. A continuous line appears down the lefthand margin showing the extent of the ruler. The line has arrowheads at each end, so you can see easily if the ruler extends beyond the text visible in the window because one or both of the arrowheads will not be shown.

Removing rulers

To remove a ruler, position the cursor somewhere in the text within its extent and use **Delete ruler** from the Layout menu. The ruler before the one you have deleted will now operate over the extent of the deleted ruler. To see the effect of the change of ruler, you will have to reformat the text using **Reformat Between rulers**.

Indents

Indents are useful if you want to set some text apart for any reason. A typical use of indents is to distinguish quotations from the main text.

To indent a paragraph you are about to type, position the cursor and use **Indent** from the Layout menu or press F9. The cursor will jump to the first tab position. As text wraps around, new lines will begin directly under the start of the first line so that all lines begin under the first tab position.

To indent a paragraph you have already typed, position the cursor on the first character of the first line and use **Indent** or press F9. The first line is then indented to the first tab position. You will need to use **Reformat** or F7 to format and indent the rest of the paragraph.

Moving on...

The next chapter explains how to edit the text you have typed.

6 Editing text

One of the great advantages of a word-processor over a typewriter is that you can change your text as many times as you like without having to retype it. You can add new bits, delete chunks, move bits around, copy sections and make global changes to words and phrases with so little effort you may find it difficult to leave your finished text alone – there's always one more little improvement you can make!

Many of the editing tasks you can perform in 1st Word Plus require you to select a chunk of text first. Selecting text was described in the previous chapter.

Using the clipboard

1st Word Plus allows you to cut or copy a piece of text and insert it elsewhere in your document or in a different document. The cut or copied text is stored temporarily in an area of the computer's memory referred to as the clipboard because it performs the same function as a physical clipboard holding a piece of text you had snipped out of a paper document. You can only store one piece of text at a time on the clipboard. If there is already some text stored, and you copy, move or delete some more text, a message appears warning you that you haven't used the text on the clipboard and are about to overwrite it. If you click on OK, the text originally stored on the clipboard will be lost. The contents of the clipboard are not lost if you close your 1st Word Plus document, but they are lost if you quit 1st Word Plus or turn the computer off. You can't look directly at the clipboard, but if you want to know what is stored on it you can use **Paste** to insert a copy of the contents of the clipboard into the document. This is described below.

Copying, moving and deleting text

Copying, moving and deleting text all use the clipboard. You must also have some text selected before these menu options are available.

To delete text, select the block you want to remove and use **Cut** from the Select menu or press Ctrl-F7. If there is anything on the clipboard when you do this, a dialogue box will appear asking if you want to overwrite the clipboard contents (OK) or cancel the operation. If there isn't anything on the clipboard at the time, the dialogue box will just tell you that the block of text has been stored on the clipboard. If the chunk you cut is too large for the clipboard, you will be given the chance to cut it anyway, though you won't be able to get it back, or to cancel the operation.

Any text you have cut and stored on the clipboard can be pasted back into the same document or a different document. To do this, place the cursor where you want to insert the text and use **Paste** from the Select menu or press Ctrl-F9. You can paste several copies of the text as it remains on the clipboard until you overwrite it by cutting or copying something else, or quit from 1st Word Plus, or turn off the computer.

To copy text, select the block you want to copy and use **Copy** from the Select menu or press Ctrl-C. The text in the document will remain as it is, but a copy will be stored on the clipboard. Again, if there is anything on the clipboard, you will be offered the chance to cancel rather than overwrite the clipboard contents. If nothing is stored on the clipboard, a message will tell you that the block has been copied to it. To add a copy of the text to the same document or a different document, place the cursor and use **Paste** or Ctrl-F9.

If you want to move a block of text from one place to another within the same document, you don't need to cut and then paste it; you can use **Move** instead. This uses the clipboard briefly, but a copy of the moved text isn't stored on the clipboard afterwards as it is with **Cut**. To move a block of text, select it and then place the cursor at the point where you want to insert the block. Use **Move** from the Select menu or press Ctrl-F10. The block is removed from its original position and inserted at the cursor position. Because this uses the clipboard momentarily, you will be asked to confirm that you want to overwrite any existing contents of the clipboard. If there is nothing on the clipboard, no message will appear. You can't paste more copies of the moved text into the document, and you can't move blocks of text between documents using this procedure – you have to use **Cut** and **Paste** for that.

Finding and replacing text

Sometimes you might want to find or replace all instances of a text string. (A text string is a word, group of words, or group of characters.) 1st Word Plus allows you to do this searching either up or down the document from the cursor position.

You will probably more often want to replace text strings than just find them. For example, if you have written a story about a boy called Robert, and you decide to change his name to Rory, you can use **Replace** for this. **Replace** and **Find** both work from the cursor position, so if you want to search through a whole document, first move the cursor to the beginning (or end) of the document. To replace one text string with another, use **Replace** from the Edit menu, or Ctrl-F3, to display the Find and replace dialogue box:

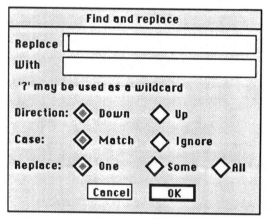

Type the text you want to replace in the first field (eg Robert) and the text you want to replace it with in the second field (eg Rory). You can use the question mark ? to stand for any character at all, so ro? in the first field would find roa, rob, roc, rod, etc and also ro1 –ro9, ro followed by a punctuation point and even ro followed by a space; strings such as 'Ron', 'Robert', 'rot', and 'hero,' would all be affected. When one character is used to stand for any other character like this it is called a *wildcard*. You might not use the wildcard on many occasions, but it is useful if you want to change, say, all references to 'D.Harris', 'P.Harris' and 'J.Harris' to 'Mr Harris' (use '??Harris').

Remember that 1st Word Plus will not check that the string appears on its own. You can end up with some quite unexpected changes because of this. If you decide to change 'man' to 'person' throughout your document, you can find later that you have also changed 'manoeuvre' to 'personoeuvre', 'demand' to 'depersond' and 'woman' to 'woperson'!

The search can be case-sensitive, or take no notice of case. If you know the string you want to change will always be in the same case, it is worth using Match as it can cut down the number of possible mistaken replacements. For example, if you want to replace 'Ron' with 'Rod', type 'Ron' and make the search match cases so that you don't also change 'electron', 'prong' and 'erroneous'. If you use Ignore, the next time the dialogue box is displayed, the text in the first field will have changed to upper-case. If you now switch to Match case using the same string, only upper-case instances will be found – 1st Word Plus won't remember the case of the string as you originally typed it.

You can choose the direction in which the document will be searched; this will be up or down from the cursor position. If the search goes all the way to the end (or start) of the document, the default search direction will be the opposite next time you display the Find and replace dialogue box. For example, if you replaced all instances of 'Robert' with 'Rory' searching down, the search would finish at the end of the document. When you next displayed the dialogue box, the direction selected automatically would be Up. This is actually quite awkward, since you usually want to search through a document in the same direction (generally downwards). You will probably find quite often that you start with the cursor at the top of a document and the search doesn't appear to work, only to discover that it was searching upwards, where there isn't any text, of course!

You can search for and replace the first instance of the text string, or All instances of it, or Some. If you choose Some, a dialogue box will appear each time 1st Word Plus finds the string; you need to choose whether to replace that instance, leave it but continue the search, or abort the search.

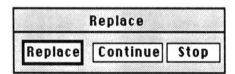

Click on the option you want to use.

A word of warning about Replace (and Find): words split with an automatic hyphen, and phrases split over a line break, are not found by either of these commands. This can be very inconvenient, and it's difficult to spot that some instances have been missed. You can run a quick check after using **Replace** by using **Find** with just the first word of a phrase (or the first letters of a word) to go through the document and check that there aren't any split across lines, but there's nothing else you can do to help with this.

Just finding text

You will probably use just **Find** (and not **Replace**) when you want to check references or text near an identifying string. For example, if you had a document which included a lot of prices, and you knew the prices had changed variously, you could search for the pound sign (£) to find all the prices and change each one to the right value.

To find a text string, use **Find** from the Edit menu or press Ctrl-F2 to display this dialogue box.

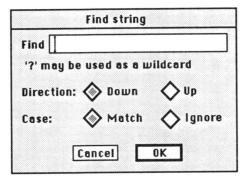

If you have used **Find** or **Replace** already, the last string you searched for will be shown in the Find field. The direction will be Down unless the last search ended at the bottom of the document. The case option will be Match unless you used Ignore for the previous search.

When you have used **Find** (but not if you last used **Replace**) you can use Repeat find in the Edit menu, or Ctrl-F1, to find the next instance of the string.

The warning about **Replace** with soft hyphens and phrases split over line breaks applies to **Find**, too.

Changing the case of text

There are two options that allow you to change the case of words. These are **Change case** and **Title**

word, both in the Select menu. You need to have selected some text to use them.

Change case switches the case of all letters in the selected block. So 'rodney' would change to 'RODNEY', and 'Dear Grandad' would change to 'dEAR gRANDAD'. You can use Ctrl-V instead of the menu option.

Title word changes the initial letter of each word in the selected block to a capital and other letters to lower-case. If the initial letter is already a capital it doesn't change. 'news of the world' would change to 'News Of The World', and both 'dEAR gRANDAD' and 'DEAR GRANDAD' would change to 'Dear Grandad'. However, 'learning to use BASIC' will be changed to the inappropriate 'Learning To Use Basic'. If a word has a character other than a space before it, such as a quotation mark or bracket, it won't be given an initial capital. You can also use Ctrl-X instead of the menu option to change the first letters of words to capitals.

Moving on...

The next chapter explains how to move around the document, which you will often need to do when you are editing your text.

7 Moving around the document

If you are using a short document, you will probably move around it using the scroll bars and cursor keys. Remember that you can use Shift with the cursor keys, and the Page Up and Page Down keys, to move up or down a screenful of text at a time, and Ctrl with the cursor keys to move to the start or end of the document. You can also place markers in the text and move to these, and go to a specified page.

Using markers

You can put up to four place markers in a document at any time. You can't see the markers, but you can use a menu option to move the cursor to one of them. This is particularly useful if there is a place in your document you keep wanting to come back to.

To place a marker, position the cursor where you want the marker to be and use **Set mark** from the Edit menu. This has a sub-menu offering markers numbered 1 to 4.

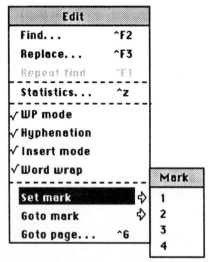

Click on the number you want to use. Unfortunately, 1st Word Plus doesn't show you which markers are already in use; you will need to remember which markers you have used and want to keep in their current place. If you click on the number of a marker already in use, that marker will be moved to the new position with no warning message and there will be no marker in its original position.

When you want to move the cursor back to the position of the marker, use **Goto mark** in the Edit menu. This also displays a sub-menu showing the numbers of the markers, but again it doesn't show which ones are in use. If you click on the number of a marker that is not set, the cursor will go to the top of the document. You can't use markers in footnotes.

Using page numbers

You can also move around the document by specifying the number of the page you want to move to. To do this, use **Goto page** in the Edit menu to display this dialogue box:

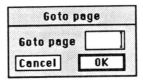

Type the number of the page you want to move to in the field and click on OK. If you leave the field blank and click on OK, the cursor will move to the top of the document.

Moving to a page specified by its number is most useful when you are correcting your document from a printed copy. The printed copy is likely to have page numbers on it, and this can help you to find the sections you want to alter.

Finding selected text

You can also move to the start or end of a selected block of text. This is described in chapter **4**: Styling text. Use the options **Find start** (or Ctrl-T) and **Find end** (or Ctrl-B) from the Select menu.

Moving on...

The next chapter explains how to control the layout of the pages in your document, adding header and footer text and controlling the length of pages and position of page breaks.

8 Page design

There are several aspects of the page design of a 1st Word Plus document that you can control. You can add headers and footers (that is, text that will appear at the top or bottom of every page), include page numbers in header and footer text, set the page length in number of lines, set the left and right margins, and control where page breaks fall.

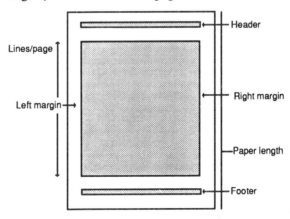

All aspects of page layout are set using the Page layout dialogue box. You control the placing of page breaks page to page as you want to, so this is not included in the dialogue box. To display the dialogue box, use Page layout in the Layout menu.

```
┌──────────────────────────────────────────────────┐
│                    Page layout                     │
├──────────────────────────────────────────────────┤
│                      Header                        │
│   Left    [ |                               ]      │
│   Centre  [                                 ]      │
│   Right   [                                 ]      │
│                      Footer                        │
│   Left    [                                 ]      │
│   Centre  [ #                               ]      │
│   Right   [                                 ]      │
│                                                    │
│   Paper length [66] ⇧ ⇩   Lines/page [54]         │
│   TOF margin   [1] ⇧ ⇩    BOF margin  [5] ⇧ ⇩     │
│   Head margin  [3] ⇧ ⇩    Foot margin [3] ⇧ ⇩     │
│                [Cancel]  [ OK ]                     │
└──────────────────────────────────────────────────┘
```

Header and footer text

A header is text that appears on the top of every page. Typical uses for headers are to give the title of a chapter or report, or the page number.

A footer is text that appears on the bottom of every page. This may include a page number and perhaps other information, such as the name of the author of a report, or the issue number.

The header and footer text can each have up to three components: text aligned with the left margin, text centred between the margins, and text aligned with the right margin.

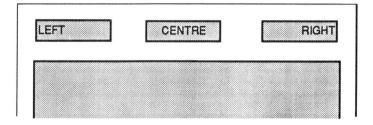

There is a field for each component of the header and footer on the dialogue box. When you first display the dialogue box, there is usually only one component set, and that is a central # as the footer. Hash (#) is used to include the page number. This will be automatically replaced by 1st Word Plus with the page number for each page when the document is printed. You can include other text in a line with a #. Examples are:

Text	Gives
Page #	Page 1, Page 2, etc
Page 4-#	Page 4-1, Page 4-2, etc
- # -	- 1 -, - 2 -, etc

You can use # in any of the header and footer areas, and you can even use it more than once if you want to.

Each component can be up to 25 characters long, though whether a header or footer with 75 characters will fit on your page depends on the paper size and text pitch you have chosen to use.

Placement of headers and footers

To set the position for headers and footers, you need to say how many lines to leave above the header and below the footer, and how many lines to leave between the header and the body text (main text of the page) and between the footer and the body text. These are set from the same dialogue box.

TOF margin is the number of lines that will be left at the top of the page before the header is printed. TOF stands for Top Of Form.

BOF margin is the number of lines that will be left blank beneath the footer. BOF stands for Bottom Of Form.

Head margin is the number of lines that will be left between the header and the body text.

Foot margin is the number of lines that will be left between the body text and the footer.

To set any of these, use the arrow icons beside the numbers. As you change these settings, the Lines/page setting will be updated automatically to show how many lines of body text will fit on the page. This is calculated by adding up all the margins and subtracting the total from the paper length. You can't set this number yourself.

Paper length

To set the paper length, you need to say how many lines will fit on the paper you are going to use. The default value is 66. This is the number of lines that will fit on an A4 page. If you want to use a different size paper, look in the manual for your printer to see how many lines will fit on the paper you want to use. If you can't find the information you need, set all the margins to zero and print out some pages with text on every line, then count the number of lines that are printed on a page. You might need to alter the settings on your printer to set TOF and BOF margins to zero. If you have the disc that accompanies this book, there is a text file of line numbers you can print out to find out how many lines fit on the page. It is called 'pagelength'.

Controlling page breaks

Normally, a page break will come when the number of lines per page has been reached. A natural page break is shown in the margin of the document like this:

Sometimes, though, you might want to force a page break where one would not naturally occur. This might be to start some new material on a new page, or to prevent 'widows' – a single line left at the bottom of a page when the rest of the paragraph is carried over to the next page.

To add a page break, position the pointer in the margin next to the line that you want to make the first line of the new page and click the lefthand mouse button. This is a 'hard' page break, and is shown like this:

The hard page break will remain, even if you edit the text so that the line you originally wanted to start a new page moves away from the page break. You might then want to remove the hard page break. To do this, click on the page number in the margin with the lefthand mouse button.

Sometimes, there may be material that you want to keep together and not have split over a page break. Instead of looking at and altering the page breaks as you edit the document, you can add a conditional page break. This is a page break that will be added at the start of the group if otherwise a page break would fall in the group of lines you have marked for keeping together. If a page break would not fall in the group, no extra page break will be added. To insert a conditional page break, position the cursor in the left margin beside the first line of the group, then press and hold down the lefthand mouse button and drag down until the pointer is beside the last line of the group. The conditional page break is shown in the margin by a horizontal broken line beside the first line of the group, and a vertical broken line extending the full length of the group.

Component prices, 1992

Code	£
A645/1	46.00
A645/2	37.50
A646	39.80

A conditional page break is a useful way of keeping text in a table together. It will remain in the same place even if you edit the text so that the group of lines falls in a different place, or is deleted. If you want to remove the conditional page break, click on the mark in the margin. You can also use conditional page breaks to prevent orphans. (An orphan is a single line a the top of a new page when the rest of the paragraph is on the previous page.) To do this, hold the last few lines of a paragraph together with a conditional page break. Be consistent in the number of lines you link, and make sure you don't end up with a lot of widows instead!

Moving on...

The next chapter explains how to set some options that control how you use 1st Word Plus and how it will behave. It covers options such as word-wrap, hyphenation, display of the rulers, and 'WP mode'.

9 Setting some options

There are several options you can set to control the way the document is displayed and treated. These form rather a miscellaneous collection. Most are set using the Edit menu, but one comes in the Layout menu.

Insert and overstrike mode

At the start of the book, we looked at the Insert key, used to switch between insert mode and overstrike mode. The option **Insert mode** in the Edit menu has the same function as this key. When insert mode is enabled, the menu option is ticked and new text you type will appear at the cursor position, pushing any text in front of the cursor forward to make space for it. When insert mode is disabled, new text will be typed over any existing text at the cursor position, replacing it. Click on the menu option or use the Insert key to switch between the two modes.

Hyphenation

When you reformat one or more paragraphs, 1st Word Plus will move complete words over on to a new line to make the line fit the margins you have set. If a long word falls at the end of a line, a dialogue box will appear giving you the option of hyphenating the word and splitting it over two lines, of carrying it over completely, or disabling hyphenation. If a word is longer than eight characters (including any punctuation points), 1st Word Plus may give you the option of hyphenating it (unless you have disabled hyphenation). If you don't want any words to be hyphenated, disable hyphenation, either using the option in the Edit menu or using the dialogue box displayed when a word could be hyphenated.

The hyphenation dialogue box shows how a word will be hyphenated if you choose to use the hyphen:

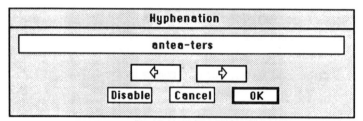

1st Word Plus uses a series of rules to help it decide where to place the hyphen, but these do not adequately cover all words. As the example above shows, it will sometimes offer a poorly-placed hyphen. You can control the position of the hyphen, moving it backwards or forwards through the word by clicking on the arrow icons. If the hyphen will not move any further to the right, that is because you already have as many letters as will fit in the line to the left of the hyphen. When you are happy with the position of the hyphen, click on OK to break the word as it is shown. If you want to carry the word over to the next line, click on Cancel. If you want to prevent any words being hyphenated, click on Disable. This alters the hyphenation setting, and hyphenation will be disabled until you use the menu option to enable it again.

When 1st Word Plus adds a hyphen it is called a 'soft' hyphen, and is shown on screen by the character ~ to distinguish it from a 'hard' hyphen that you have typed (-). A soft hyphen is printed with an ordinary hyphen character. The soft hyphen will only be used if the word falls over a line break, otherwise it will not appear on screen or when you print out the document. If you later import your document into a desktop publishing package, the soft hyphens will be discarded.

Hyphenation is never added as you type. If a word is too long to fit on the line, it will be carried over to the next line. If you want to use hyphenation to gain the optimum word-spacing through lines and the minimum white space on the page, reformat your work after you have typed it.

Unfortunately, you can't remove hyphenation by turning it off and then reformatting the text. This means that you can't reformat the text to get around the problem of **Find, Replace** and **Check spelling** failing to recognise words that have been hyphenated. If you really want to get rid of the hyphens, you'll have to reformat using a different ruler and with hyphenation turned off, then go back to the original ruler and reformat again. This is really only feasible if you have only used one ruler throughout the document.

Show position and show ruler

By default, the current ruler for the cursor position is shown along the top of the window. There is an option in the Layout menu, **Show ruler**, that allows you to turn the display of the ruler on and off. You can also use the keystroke Ctrl-L. When the ruler is turned off, the text starts immediately at the top of the window.

If you prefer, you can see a report of your position in the document in place of the ruler. This shows the page, line and column (character position) number, and is constantly updated as you type. Use the option **Show position** in the Layout menu or Ctrl-P to turn this on.

```
┌──────────────────────────────────────────┐
│ ▚    Page 2 Line 31 Column 23             │
└──────────────────────────────────────────┘
```

You can't display the ruler and position at the same time. If you turn on the position, the ruler will be replaced and vice versa. You can turn both off, in which case the line below the title bar that shows the ruler or position will disappear completely.

Word wrap

Word wrap is the facility that allows text to jump to the next line when your typing reaches the righthand margin. Word wrap is turned on when you start up 1st Word Plus. If you want to turn it off, click on **Word wrap** in the Edit menu to remove the tick. If you turn word wrap off, you will be able to carry on typing beyond the end of the ruler you have set, up to a maximum line of 160 characters.

WP mode

WP mode stands for 'word-processor mode' and is the mode in which you will probably use 1st Word

Plus most. It means that 1st Word Plus will store information relating to its use as a word-processing program in each file, keeping a record of all the special effects and layout options you have used. When you save a file using WP mode, information about bold, italic and other effects, headers and footers, padding spaces and soft hyphens is stored so that when you re-load the file later it is exactly as you left it. If you turn WP mode off, this information is discarded when you save the file. Instead, the file is saved just as ASCII text – text with no information about it as a word-processed document.

ASCII text is an international standard used for porting text between different systems, programs and computers. ASCII stands for American Standard Character for Information Interchange. You will need to save your document as ASCII text if you want to transfer it to a PC system, for example, or if you have written the text of a program in 1st Word Plus. When you use 1st Word Plus in WP mode, it stores various codes and markers within the document which 1st Word Plus itself understands and interprets. Acorn Desktop Publisher and Impression also understand these codes and retain the special text effects you have added. Other programs, though, use the same codes for different things, or don't recognise the codes at all, so they need just the text. When you save a document without using WP mode, all the codes and markers are discarded and only the text characters are retained in the file. When you save a 1st Word Plus document with WP mode turned off, the result is an Edit file, with an Edit file icon. This is because Edit produces ASCII text files. You can see how 1st Word Plus adds extra codes to a document for its processing if you drag a 1st Word Plus document icon into an Edit window. The following three diagrams show the same piece of text in 1st Word Plus (1) and then dragged into an Edit window when saved with WP mode turned on (2) and with it turned off (3).

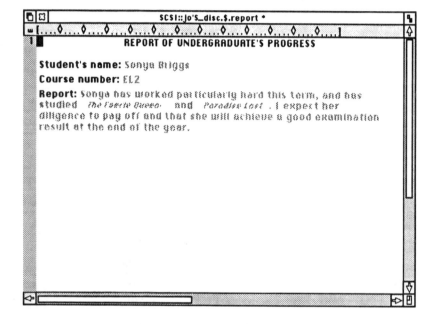

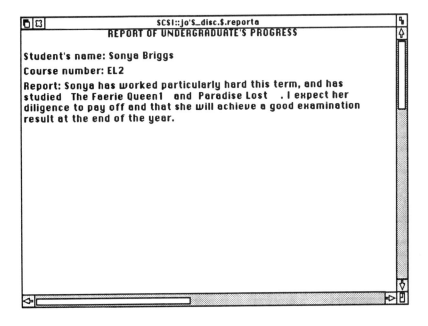

```
┌──────────────────────────────────────────────────────┐
│ ▣▣            SCSI::Jo'S_disc.$.report              ▐ │
│ [1f]066010305800                                       │
│ [1f]1[1f][1f]                                          │
│ [1f]2[1f]#[1f]                                          │
│ [1f]F0110030                                           │
│ [1f]R  [.[7f]....[7f]....[7f]....[7f]....[7f]....[7f]....[7f]....│
│ [7f]....[7f]....[7f]....[7f]....[7f]....]011            │
│ [1f]9[....[7f]....[7f]....[7f]....[7f]....[7f]....[7f]....[7f]....│
│ [7f]....[7f]....[7f]....[7f]....]011                    │
│ [1b] [1d][1c][1c][1c][1c][1c][1c][1c][1c][1c][1c][1c][1c][1c]REPO│
│ RTC1e]OF[1e]UNDERGRADUATE'S[1e]PROGRESS                 │
│ [1b]√                                                   │
│                                                        │
│ [1b]☐Student's[1e]name:[1b]√[1e]Sonya[1e]Briggs        │
│                                                        │
│ [1b]☐Course[1e]number:[1b]√[1e]EL2                     │
│                                                        │
│ [1b]☐Report:[1b]√[1e][1c]Sonya[1e][1c]has[1e]worked[1e]particularly│
│ [1e]hard[1e]this[1e]term, [1e][1c]and[1e][1c]has[1e]    │
│ [0b][11]studied[1e][1c][1b]☐The[1e][1c]Faerie[1e][1c]Queen[1b]. [18]01│
│ ,1[18][1b]√[1e][1c]and[1e][1c][1b]☐Paradise[1e][1c]Lost[1b]√.[1e][1c]│
│ I[1e][1c]expect[1e][1c]her[1e]                          │
│ diligence[1e]to[1e]pay[1e]off[1e]and[1e]that[1e]she[1e]will[1e]achiev│
│ e[1e]a[1e]good[1e]examination[1e]                        │
│ result[1e]at[1e]the[1e]end[1e]of[1e]the[1e]year.        │
│                                                        │
│ [1f]N001:002700080001                                   │
│ [1b]√[1d][1c][1c]The[1e]text[1e]is[1e]taught[1e]in[1e]it's[1e]entirety│
│ [1e]using[1e]the[1e]OUP[1e]edition.                     │
│ [1f]E                                                   │
└──────────────────────────────────────────────────────┘
```

```
┌──────────────────────────────────────────────────────┐
│ ▣▣            SCSI::Jo'S_disc.$.reporta             ▐ │
│ REPORT OF UNDERGRADUATE'S PROGRESS                     │
│                                                        │
│ Student's name: Sonya Briggs                           │
│ Course number: EL2                                     │
│ Report: Sonya has worked particularly hard this term, and has│
│ studied  The Faerie Queen1  and  Paradise Lost  . I expect her│
│ diligence to pay off and that she will achieve a good examination│
│ result at the end of the year.                         │
└──────────────────────────────────────────────────────┘
```

When WP mode is turned on, 1st Word Plus adds some header text which identifies the file as a 1st Word Plus document. This runs from the start of the file to the code [1b] before the title that you can see in the second illustration. 1st Word Plus distinguishes between two types of spaces: the hard spaces you type and the soft spaces added to pad lines when you reformat a paragraph. These are stored as the hexadecimal codes [1e] and [1c] respectively in the first file. When WP mode is turned off, this distinction is lost and all the spaces are identified by the ASCII space character. Other codes in the WP mode file indicate the start and end of bold or italic text, the beginning of the footnote, and the end of the file. With WP mode turned off, these markers are discarded, and the footnote is lost.

Even if you want eventually to save your document with WP mode turned off because you want to transfer it to another system or use it as a program, it is easiest to work with WP mode turned on. If you turn off WP mode, these changes will affect your work

- you can't use word wrap, but will have to press Return at the end of each line

- you won't be able to reformat the text

- the special effects (such as bold and italic) won't work

- you won't be able to change or add rulers

- page design options won't be available

- you won't be able to add page breaks

- you won't be able to add footnotes

- you can't use automatic hyphenation (which is added only when you reformat the text)

◆   the **Goto page** option in the Edit menu
turns to **Goto line**.

Some of these changes won't matter, because special
effects, headers and footers, and footnotes won't be
carried across to a different system or used in a
program anyway. However, it is often useful to be
able to print out your work with page numbers on
it, to reformat it so that it remains tidy, and to use
special text effects temporarily to help you find your
way around the document while you work on it,
even though these will all be lost when you save the
text as an ASCII file. It is best to work in WP mode,
and save your final version of the document with
WP mode turned off.

Moving on...

The next chapter explains how to use footnotes in
your document.

10 Using footnotes

You can add footnotes to a 1st Word Plus document and control where the footnotes are positioned on the page. Footnotes are generally used for holding textual references and sometimes for material that is of interest and relevance but does not form part of the main argument of the text.

Adding a footnote

When you want to add a footnote, position the cursor where you want the superscript number for the footnote to appear and use **Add footnote** from the Layout menu or press Ctrl-F4. A separate window opens for you to type the text of the footnote.

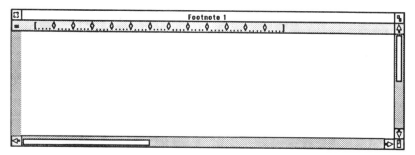

The cursor is at the left edge of the window, although the ruler leaves a small left margin. When you begin to type, the text will appear at the first position as shown by the ruler.

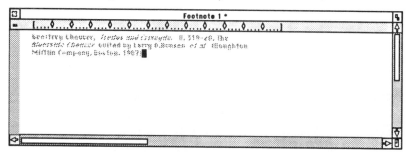

The space remaining at the left will hold the footnote number when the document is printed. You can alter the ruler in the footnote, use special text effects and use centred or right-aligned text, but you can't include graphics in a footnote.

When you have finished typing text for the footnote, close the footnote window. A superscript number will appear in the text at the position of the footnote reference. The footnote numbers are automatically incremented, the next number being used each time you add a footnote. If you add a footnote at any point before the last one in the document, the later footnotes will be renumbered to accommodate the additional one.

You can't see the footnote text on the page when you have the document on screen. If you want to check the text of a footnote without printing out the document, or if you want to alter the text in the footnote, double-click on the footnote reference number in the text to display the footnote window. You can edit footnote text in the same way as any other text.

If you have more than 255 footnotes in a document, or try to use a footnote which is more than a page long, the document will be corrupted when you save it and you won't be able to use it properly in future. You are unlikely to reach these limits, but they are worth bearing in mind.

Layout of footnotes

Footnotes are printed at the bottom of the page on which their footnote reference number appears. You can control how much space is left above and below the footnote, and how long a rule is used to divide the footnote from the text when the document is printed out.

Use **Footnote format** in the Layout menu to display this dialogue box:

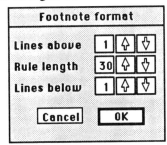

You can type directly in the fields, or use the arrows to increase or decrease the values.

Unless you reduce the length of the rule to zero, a horizontal rule will be printed to separate the footnotes from the body text on the page. The length of the rule is measured in character spaces.

The space above and below the footnotes is measured in lines.

Editing text containing footnotes

You can edit text containing footnotes just as you can edit any other text. If your editing rearranges the text so that the footnotes fall in a different sequence, they will be automatically renumbered. If you try to delete any text which contains a footnote reference, a dialogue box appears asking you to confirm that you want to delete the footnotes. If you do delete the text and footnotes, the other footnotes are renumbered to take account of the change. If you click on Cancel, neither the text nor the footnotes will be deleted.

It is worth remembering that if you use **Find** or **Replace** in text with footnotes, you will be offered the option of continuing the search into the footnotes only if the search direction is forward. This means that if you have text with footnotes and you want to do several replacements, you ought to move the cursor up to the start of the document and change the search direction to Down each time; if you don't, you might miss some instances you wanted to replace that occur in the footnotes.

You can reformat text in a footnote with that footnote open and using **Reformat** or F7 within the window, or if you use **Reformat Whole document** the footnotes will be reformatted. **Reformat Between rulers** doesn't reformat the footnotes between the rulers, though.

Importing footnote text

You can prepare the text for footnotes in a separate document and drag the file – or paste copied or cut text – into the footnote window. There is no point in doing this if you are creating a new document with footnotes in it, but if you are converting text you already have to a 1st Word Plus document you might need to do this to avoid retyping the footnotes.

To paste text into a footnote, copy or cut the text so that it is stored on the clipboard, open the footnote window and use Ctrl-F9 or Paste to insert the text. Chapter 13: Using several documents at once explains in detail how to move text around between documents.

You can drag a file icon into the footnote window to add the whole text from that file to the footnote.

If you use either of these methods for adding text to a footnote, the footnote text will start at the extreme left, that is, off the left of the footnote ruler. You will need to use Reformat or Ctrl-F7 to reformat the text in the footnote, otherwise the footnote number will be overwritten when the text is printed.

Moving on...

The next chapter explains how to use the 1st Word Plus spelling checker.

11 Checking your spelling

1st Word Plus has a spelling check facility to help
you make sure your work is free from spelling errors.
It has a main dictionary, and you can build up your
own supplementary dictionaries too.

Using the spelling checker

When you start up 1st Word Plus, the spelling
checker dictionary is not loaded. You need to load it
before you can check the spelling in your document.
Use **Load dictionary** in the Spelling sub-menu.
After a little disc activity, the dictionary is loaded.
The other options in the Spelling sub-menu then
become available:

```
┌─────────────────────────────────────┐
│          Spelling                    │
├─────────────────────────────────────┤
│ Load dictionary                      │
│ ─ ─ ─ ─ ─ ─ ─ ─ ─ ─ ─ ─ ─ ─ ─ ─ ─    │
│ Check Spelling              ESC      │
│ Continuous spelling                  │
│ Browse...                   ^F5      │
│ Add word                    ^F6      │
│ End spell check                      │
└─────────────────────────────────────┘
```

You can use the spelling checker in either of two ways. You can set it to check your spelling all the time, as you type, or you can check through a document after you have typed it.

If you want 1st Word Plus to check your spelling as you type, click on **Continuous spelling**. As you type, 1st Word Plus compares each word (taken to be a group of characters followed by a space or a punctuation point) with the words in its dictionary. If it doesn't find the word in its dictionary, a beep sounds warning you that the spelling is (or at least may be) incorrect. You might find this rather annoying, as it will beep at most proper names and some common abbreviations and shortened forms of words. When you hear a beep, you can carry on typing regardless, or correct the spelling if the word really is misspelled. The options are described further below.

If you don't want to check the spellings as you type, you can run through the whole document looking for spelling errors after you have typed it. Again, a beep will sound each time a word not in the dictionary is found and you can change the spelling if it is wrong. To check through a document, place the cursor at the start and use **Check spelling** from the Spelling menu or press the Escape key (to the left of the function keys). This moves the cursor to the first word that isn't found in the dictionary. If you want to accept the word as it is, press Escape or use **Check spelling** again to move to the next word that doesn't appear in the dictionary.

When 1st Word Plus finds a word that isn't in the dictionary, there are two possibilities:

◆   you have misspelled the word, or

◆   the word is correctly spelled, but isn't in the dictionary.

If you are not sure whether you have spelled the word correctly, use **Browse** from the Spelling menu, or press Ctrl-F5. This displays a window onto the dictionary:

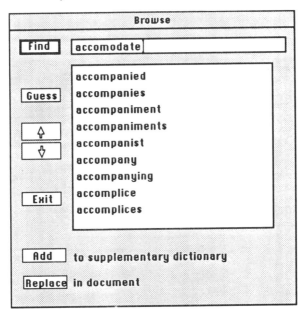

The words visible in the window are those that would come after the word you typed if it were in the dictionary. This is rather confusing; it means that about half the time, the word you really want will not be shown as it comes before the position your misspelling would occupy. If you can't see the word you want, click on the up or down arrow to move the dictionary through the window. In the example shown above, the correct spelling, accommodate, comes before the position accomodate would occupy, so you would need to move up through the dictionary. If you see the word you want, click on it to highlight it:

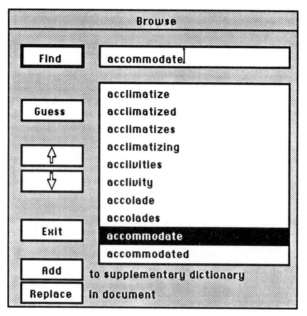

Then click on **Replace** to replace your misspelling with the correctly spelled word. The word will be replaced and the browser window will disappear.

If you can't see the word you want, but think it should be in the dictionary, click on **Guess**. 1st Word Plus will then try to match the word you typed letter for letter with others in the dictionary (rather than just looking at its alphabetical placing) and 'guess' which word you intended. It displays the chosen word in the window.

If this is the word you want, click on **Replace**. Sometimes, it will display more than one word if by changing one letter you could make two acceptable words:

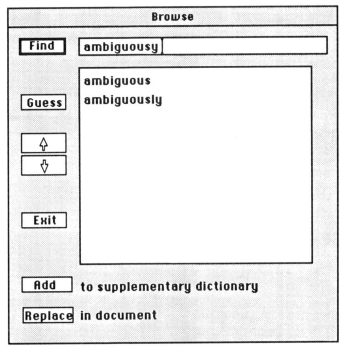

Click on the word you want, and then on **Replace**. Occasionally, **Guess** may find no acceptable words.

Sometimes, you may find that the word you want isn't in the dictionary at all. You can then click on **Exit** to get back to the document without altering the spelling you used, or you can add the word to a supplementary dictionary (with **Add**) and then use **Exit**.

The spelling checker ignores punctuation points and numbers, so if you have inadvertently used one of these in a word, but the word is otherwise correctly spelled, the check won't pick it up. This means that misspellings like 'pos6ter' and 't5ree' will be missed.

Using supplementary dictionaries

A supplementary dictionary is a dictionary built up from spellings you have used that are not found in the main dictionary. Typically, this will contain proper names that you use a lot and that you don't want the spelling checker to pick up as errors each time you use them. Default supplementary dictionary is loaded each time you load the main dictionary. If you choose to add any words, they are copied into this dictionary. You can then save your supplementary dictionary, if you want to, for later use or to merge with the main dictionary so that your words will always be recognised in future. Once you have created a supplementary dictionary, you can save it and reload it in the future.

When 1st Word Plus finds a spelling which it can't match with a word from the main dictionary or the current supplementary dictionary, you can add the word to your supplementary dictionary. To do this, use **Add word** in the Spelling menu, or press Ctrl-F6. The word will then be accepted if it is encountered again in the same 1st Word Plus session. Before you add a word to the supplementary dictionary, be sure that you have spelled it correctly and that it doesn't happen to be the same as a common misspelling of another word. For example, if you have to write frequently to someone called Mr Teh, don't add his name to the supplementary dictionary because each time you mistype 'the' as 'teh' the spelling checker will accept the spelling.

If you do work of several kinds that involves using different vocabularies of special terms and names, you can build up a series of supplementary dictionaries. You can then load the supplementary dictionary appropriate to the work you are going to do, and know that any terms or names you have used before will be accepted, and any extras you want to add will be added to the right supplementary dictionary. Keeping separate dictionaries for different areas of your work cuts down the likelihood of a word that is correct in one context being accepted when it is actually a misspelling in another context.

When you have been adding words to a supplementary dictionary during your session, be sure to use **End spell check** from the Spelling menu or **Quit** from the icon bar menu to close 1st Word Plus when you have finished working. Both display a dialogue box warning you that you have added words to the supplementary dictionary and giving you the chance to save it. If you choose to save it, a standard save icon appears with a default name. If you use the default name, this will overwrite the existing supplementary dictionary (which may be empty). As the words originally in the dictionary have been loaded into memory, these will be saved too, so they won't be lost. If you are planning to build up a series of supplementary dictionaries suitable for different areas of your work, it is a good idea to give another name to the dictionary before you save it.

Unless you have loaded a different supplementary dictionary, the default name for saving the supplementary dictionary is 1wp_sup. This is stored inside the 1st Word Plus application directory, and is the dictionary that is loaded if you don't choose another. (To see the contents of an application directory, hold down the Shift key while you double-click on its icon.) If you use this name, the words you have added will be in the supplementary dictionary that is automatically loaded when you load the main dictionary (using **Load dictionary**).

Loading supplementary dictionaries

You can load one or more supplementary dictionaries you have previously saved by dragging their icons onto the DIC icon on the 1st Word Plus keypad window.

☐ F1 Bold	☐ F3 Italic	☐ F5 Super	F7 Reformat	F9 Indent	F11 Centre	
☐ F2 Under	☐ F4 Light	☐ F6 Sub	F8 Del line	F10 Fixed Sp	F12 Command	
☀ Insert	☐ Caps Lock			Delete ⇧	Delete ⇩	
Port:	Parallel Port	Print file		Tab	Return	
Device:	Standard backspacing printer			Space		

1st Word Plus

If you load more than one dictionary, the default name you will be offered when you come to save your added words will be the name of the last supplementary dictionary you loaded.

Editing supplementary dictionaries

Sometimes, you may accidentally add a word to a supplementary dictionary that is actually misspelled. You can remove it (or any other words you want to be flagged as misspellings).

To edit a supplementary dictionary, load it into 1st Word Plus or Edit. If you just double-click on its icon, it won't load as a 1st Word Plus document as it has the wrong type of icon. Drag the file icon onto the 1st Word Plus or Edit icon on the icon bar. The words in the supplementary dictionary appear as a list.

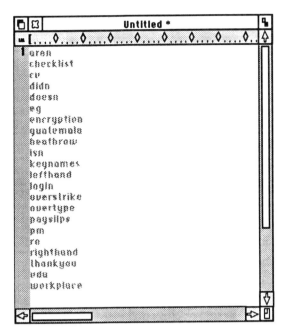

You can delete any words you don't want, or change any spellings that are wrong (though if the correctly spelled word is likely to be in the main dictionary, you may as well delete the word instead of correcting it).

When you want to save your edited dictionary, the file icon will be that of a 1WPDict file. Type the name you want to use and save the document in the usual way. It is ready for use as a supplementary dictionary.

If instead of dragging the file icon onto the 1st Word Plus or Edit icon on the icon bar you dragged the file into an empty document, the file icon you will be offered when you come to save the file is a 1st Word Plus or text file icon. Save the file with the name you want to use, and then use Settype to change the file type to 1WPDict. If you are using RISC OS 2, press F12 to go to the command line and then type:

```
settype pathname 1wpdict
```

for example,

```
settype :0.$.!1stWord+ .1wp_sup 1wpdict
```

Press Return at the end of the line, and then again to return to the desktop. The file will now have a 1WPDict icon and you can load it as a supplementary dictionary.

If you are using RISC OS 3, you can change the file type from the desktop. Open a directory display for the file and select it. Now choose **File filename Set type** from the menu. Delete the text in the writable field and type the filetype 1WPDict, then press the Return key.

Merging dictionaries

Sometimes you might want to add the words in the supplementary dictionary to the main dictionary. A program called 1stDMerge is supplied on the 1st Word Plus Program disc to enable you to do this.

If the words you have added to the supplementary dictionary do not relate to a special application or area of use but are just words that aren't in the main dictionary, you can add them to the main dictionary. It is best to build up quite a large supplementary dictionary and do this only occasionally as the process can take quite a while. If you want to merge several supplementary dictionaries with the main dictionary, it is quicker to merge the supplementary dictionaries first and then merge a single large one with the main dictionary than to merge each with the main dictionary in turn. Merging with the main dictionary is the slowest part of the process.

When you want to merge dictionaries, make sure you have directory displays on screen for the main dictionary and the supplementary dictionary you want to use, then double-click on !1stDMerge. The icon looks like this:

!1stDMerge

1stDMerge does not load with an icon on the icon bar; instead the 1stDMerge dialogue box appears:

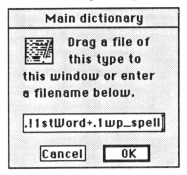

If you want to use the main dictionary, called 1wp_spell, leave the text in the field as it is. If you want to use another main dictionary, drag its text file icon to the dialogue box or type its full pathname in the field. Click on OK to display the next dialogue window:

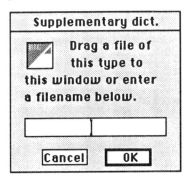

This time, you need to use a file with file type 1WPDict. It will be a supplementary dictionary file. Drag a file icon to the dialogue box or type a full pathname and then click on OK. A save icon appears for you to give the name of the new main dictionary that will be created by the merging process. You can re-save it as 1 wp_spell if you wish, and this will then be loaded as the main dictionary when you use the spelling checker. However, you might want to give it a different name initially so that you can make a copy of the original main dictionary rather than overwriting it.

When you have given a pathname or dragged the icon to a directory viewer, the merging begins. A window appears on screen reporting the progress of the merge.

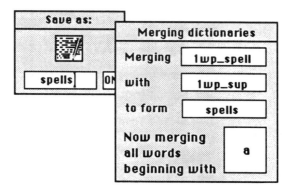

When it has finished, a dialogue box tells you that the process is complete and that the new dictionary has been created.

In order to use your new main dictionary, you must give it the name 1wp_spell. You must save the new 1wp_spell inside the !1stWord+ application directory. It is a good idea to make a copy of the original 1wp_spell first.

Removing words from the main dictionary

You might occasionally want to remove words from the main dictionary if, for example, you have accidentally merged a supplementary dictionary with it that contained a spelling error, or you find that a word in the dictionary coincides with a frequent misspelling which is consequently not found by the spelling checker.

To remove words from the main dictionary, you need to make up a special file of the words you want to remove. You can use 1st Word Plus or Edit to create the file. You must type each word you want to remove on a different line and precede each by a minus sign (hyphen: -).

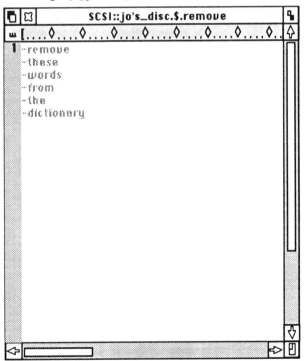

The minus sign tells 1stDMerge to remove rather than add the word when merging the file with the main dictionary. If you are using 1st Word Plus to create the file, you must turn off WP mode before you save the file. 1stDMerge will accept a text file, but not a 1st Word Plus document file as a supplementary dictionary.

When you have created your file of words to remove, use 1stDMerge as usual, dragging your text file to the second dialogue box. Although the dialogue box specifically asks for a file with the 1WPDict icon, it will also accept a text file (with the Edit icon).

Moving on...

The next chapter explains how to use pictures in your 1st Word Plus documents.

12 | Using graphics

You can include graphics in 1st Word Plus documents and print them out if you have a suitable printer. (You can't print graphics using a daisywheel printer or an HP LaserJet II printer.) This chapter explains how to include graphics in your 1st Word Plus documents.

Preparing pictures

The graphics must be in the form of a sprite (Paint) file. You can prepare the graphics in Paint, or another program that produces files of the same format. You can't use a Draw file.

When you have prepared a picture to use in a 1st Word Plus document, copy it onto the same disc, and preferably the same directory, as the document you are going to add it to. 1st Word Plus stores a reference to the pictures in a document, rather making its own copy of a picture. If it can't find the pictures referred to, it won't be able to include them when you next load the document. For this reason, you need to keep the pictures on the same disc, and not move or rename them after importing them into a document.

Importing pictures

When you want to import a picture into your document, place the cursor on the line where you want the picture to start. Now drag the file icon into the 1st Word Plus document window. The picture will appear at the position of the cursor; any text on the line will be forced down until it is beneath the picture.

If there is a 1st Word Plus printer driver loaded, the picture will have a dotted line around it to show how much space it will take up when printed out.

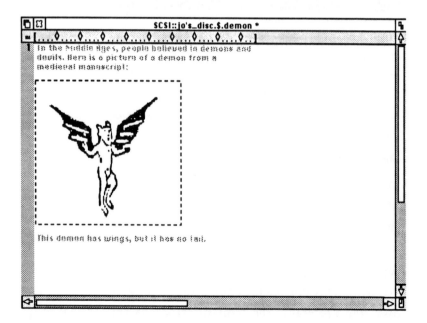

Text and pictures

When you import a picture, 1st Word Plus adds blank lines to put behind the picture. However, you can type over the picture if you like, so that your text is superimposed on it. You can use this to create some special effects:

COME TO MAXINE'S PARTY

8pm, Monday 29 September

Bring a friend!

47 Hillside, Waldebury

Tel. 78132

To type over a picture, just move the cursor to the start of the line you want to use, and begin typing (or use Tab and space bar to move across the picture to where you want to start typing). You can use all the usual special effects, such as bold, italic and centred text.

If you want to set your text to the right of a picture, you can adjust the ruler or indent the text.

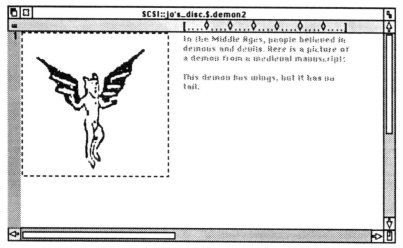

If you want to set your text to the left of a picture, you will need to shorten the ruler and move the picture over to the right.

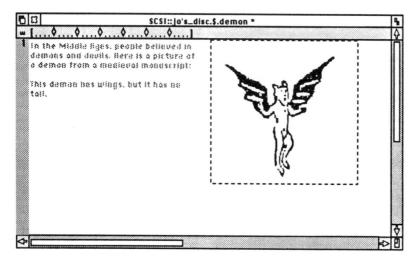

You can add extra lines above or below the picture by positioning the cursor and pressing the Return key.

Moving pictures

You can reposition a picture in your document. You may need to do this if you are adding text after you have imported the picture. If you want your text to the left or right of the picture, you will need to move the picture as the text will move to be below the picture when you drag its file in.

To move a picture, put the pointer over the area occupied by the picture (within the dotted line) and hold down the lefthand mouse button. A hand icon appears. You can now drag the picture around the document window. As you move it, a copy of the dotted outline moves around to show you the current position of the picture. You can move it so that it superimposes existing text.

You can overlay one picture on another by dragging two or more pictures into the document and then moving them around until you have the arrangement you want.

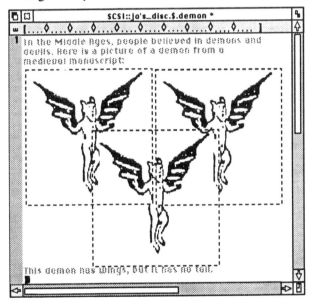

When you have several pictures overlaid, it is not always easy to move the one you want. If you position the pointer so that it is within the dotted outline of more than one picture, you won't be able to control which one is picked up. You might have to move one out of the way so that you can then move the other to where you want it.

It is possible to move your picture to the right of the ruler and then be unable to move it back again. If you move a picture so far to the right that no part of it is visible when you have the lefthand margin visible in the window, you won't be able to get it back because each time you try to place the pointer inside the picture and press the lefthand mouse button, the cursor jumps back to the lefthand margin and the window adjusts to show the margin, so the picture springs out of view again. If you have already made the window as wide as the screen allows, there is little you can do about this. If you can still make the window wider, do so and pull the picture back. If there are any screen modes you can use that you know allow a wider window, you can try using a different screen mode and picking up the picture that way. However, if you can't do either of these, you need to:

1. Create a new ruler inside the extent of the picture with the righthand margin extending into the space occupied by the picture. You will need to use the scroll bar along the bottom of the window to scroll over to the right and drag the] marker at the righthand end of the ruler until it is above the picture.

1. Type some text so that it appears over the picture – it can just be a row of dots. (You can type a very long line, or move the left margin across as well as the right margin.)

3. Put the cursor somewhere in the text that superimposes the picture. You will now be able to hold down the lefthand mouse button and select

the picture, then move it back to the left of the window.

4. Delete the text you have typed and reset the ruler to normal, or delete the extra ruler.

Pictures and text selections

You can copy or move selected text onto a picture, but it is not possible to select text superimposed on a picture. When you try to do this, the picture will move instead, as you are dragging with the lefthand mouse button inside the picture's dotted outline. You will have to move the picture first, then select the text, and then move the picture back when you have finished the text operations.

You can select pictures, or pictures and text, in the same way as you can select just text. You can then move, delete or copy and paste the pictures and text in the same document or in another document.

Reformatting text with pictures

If you have moved a picture so that it superimposes text and you then reformat the text, the picture will be moved to the end of a paragraph. You have to watch out for this, as it can result in pictures being moved so that they fall across page breaks.

Printing pictures

If you have a suitable printer driver loaded, you can print your pictures. If you have a colour printer, the colours will be reproduced as accurately as possible.

Before you print text with pictures, check that none of your pictures falls across a page break. If this happens, part of the picture is then printed on one page, and part on the next. You can avoid this by using conditional page breaks to hold each picture together. Put the pointer in the lefthand margin next to the top of the picture, press and hold down the lefthand mouse button and drag to the bottom of the picture. If a page break would have fallen inside the extent of the area you have indicated, it will occur at the start instead: all of the picture will then be printed on the next page. If a page break would not have occurred in the picture, none is added.

Deleting pictures

You can remove a picture completely from your document using the option **Delete picture** in the Graphics sub-menu. You can only use this if the cursor is inside the dotted outline of a picture. The picture is highlighted in reverse colours and you are asked to confirm that you want to delete the picture.

If you click on OK, the picture will be removed. It is not stored on the clipboard; if you want to reinstate it, you will have to copy it in again. When you delete a picture using this method, blank lines remain in the document in the space the picture occupied. You will have to delete these by selecting them and using **Cut** in the Select menu or Ctrl-F7.

If you select text including a picture and delete it, you will not be asked to confirm that you want to delete the picture. If you have graphics mode turned off so that the pictures are not displayed, be careful not to delete pictures accidentally like this.

Graphics mode

When you copy a picture into your document, 1st Word Plus automatically turns on graphics mode so that the picture can be displayed. The options in the Graphics sub-menu then become available. If you want to prevent the display of graphics in a document, click on **Graphics mode** in the menu to turn it off. This saves memory and accelerates screen redraws. The pictures remain in your document and the outline is still shown so that you do not accidentally type over the picture. When you print your document, the pictures will be printed out, even if you have graphics mode turned off.

Moving on...

The next chapter explains how to use several 1st Word Plus documents at once.

13 Using several documents at once

You can have up to four 1st Word Plus document windows open at any time, and can move or copy text and pictures between documents.

Opening multiple documents

To open several documents, you don't need to load more than one copy of 1st Word Plus. In fact, if you do load the program more than once, you won't be able to move text between documents opened with the different copies of the program.

To open more than one new document, click on the 1st Word Plus icon on the icon bar once for each new document you want to open. To open existing documents, double-click on the icon of each document in its directory display. You can open a combination of new and existing documents.

There is a default size, position and shape for each document you open.

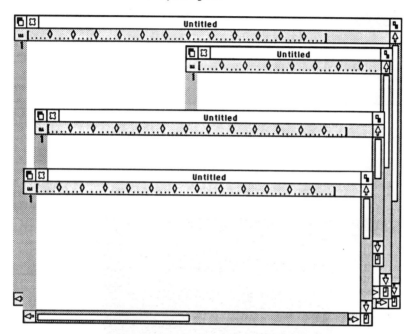

If you alter the size, shape or position, the new settings will be remembered when you close the document(s) and re-used next time you open the same number of documents. For example, if you made the document window for the second document as wide as the whole screen, but very short, then closed the document, the next time you opened a second document in the same session it would also appear in a wide, short window.

When you have more than one document open at once, only one will be active at a time. This is the one in which text will appear if you start typing. The active window has a flashing cursor and yellow title bar. The other windows have a static cursor and a grey title bar. To make the window you want to use active, click in it with the lefthand mouse button.

Moving and copying text between documents

If you want to move or copy text between documents, you can do it with both documents on screen. Open a window for each. Click in the window you want to copy or move text from to activate it. You can now select text (and pictures) in this window and delete or copy it. The selection is added to the clipboard. Now click in another document window to activate that one. The title bar goes yellow, and the cursor flashes. Position the cursor where you want to insert the text and use **Paste text**, or Ctrl-F9. The selection from the clipboard is pasted in at the cursor position.

Copy, **Cut** and **Paste** operate in the same way between documents as within a document, but you can't use **Move** to transfer selections between documents. If you want to move text from one document to another, delete it from the first document with **Cut** and then use **Paste** to add it to another document.

Moving on...

The next chapter explains how to save your document, or a block of selected text.

14 Saving your work

It is important to save your work regularly, even if you haven't finished working on your document. If you do this, you won't lose too much if you accidentally delete a large chunk of text or quit 1st Word Plus, or if a machine or power failure causes you to lose the file.

You can save the whole of your document, or a block of selected text.

Saving a document

To save a whole document, use **File** from the Save sub-menu. This displays a standard RISC OS save dialogue box. If you have previously saved the document, the icon will show the document's full pathname. You can save the document with the same name by clicking on OK. If it is a new document, the icon will show that it is 'untitled'. Delete the text in the field and type the name you want to use. You can also delete the text and type a new name if it is an existing document, but you want to save it with a different name. When the field is empty, you can type just a short name, such as 'Letter3', or a full pathname, such as 'adfs::0.$.Letters.Letter3'. If you type a short name, you need to have open a directory display for the directory in which you want to save the document. Drag the file icon into the directory display to save the document. If you type a full pathname, you can click on OK or press the Return key to save the document.

If you are saving a previously saved document with the same name, or if a document already exists with the name you choose, 1st Word Plus will ask you to confirm that you want to proceed and overwrite the original copy.

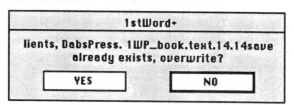

If you want to keep the original copy, click on Cancel and either choose another name for the file you are saving, or rename the existing file.

Saving a block of text

Sometimes you might want to save a block of selected text from your document as a new document in its own right. To do this, select the block of text, including pictures if you like, and use **Selection** from the Save sub-menu. The save icon won't have a default name. Supply a name for the file in the usual way. If you give a full pathname, you can click on OK or press the Return key to save the new file. If you type just a filename, drag the file icon to a directory display to save the new document. The selection will be saved as a new document, with the usual 1st Word Plus document icon. It won't make any difference that is was saved as a selection from another document.

If you save a selection, the selected text remains in the original document as well as existing as a new document on its own. If you change the new document or the original selection, the changes won't affect the other copy.

Saving ASCII text

You might sometimes want to save text you have created using 1st Word Plus as plain ASCII text with no special effects or formatting features. ASCII text can be ported to non-Acorn systems, such as PC packages, if you have the right software. You also need to save the text of any computer programs you write in 1st Word Plus as ASCII text – a program won't run if you save it as a 1st Word Plus document.

To save a document or selection as plain text, turn WP mode off (click on **WP mode** in the Edit sub-menu to remove the tick beside this option). When you use either of the Save options now, the save icon will show an Edit file icon, not a 1st Word Plus document. When you save the file, a dialogue box will appear, warning you that the document will be saved as a plain text. Click on OK to proceed.

If you save a document as a plain text file, you can't open it as a 1st Word Plus document again. You will be able to edit it in 1st Word Plus, but not use the word-processing features such as word-wrap, text styling and formatting options. If you save a document as ASCII text and later decide that you want it as a 1st Word Plus document, you can convert it by adding a suitable chunk of text as a header to start the file. This is described in chapter 18: Using 1st Word Plus with other programs.

Problems with saving files

If 1st Word Plus has difficulty saving the file, it will display this dialogue box:

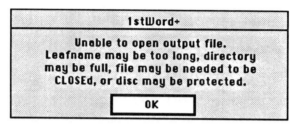

This isn't very helpful as it doesn't tell you exactly what is wrong. It can be any of the following problems:

♦ the filename is too long (it may have up to ten characters)

♦ the filename contains illegal characters, such as comma (,) or space ( )

♦ you have included in a pathname the name of a directory that doesn't exist on the disc you are using, or you have dragged the file icon to a directory display for a directory that isn't on the disc you are using

♦ the disc is write-protected

♦ you don't have write-access to the file

♦ there is no disc in the disc drive you have specified

◆ the file or directory is open (Files can be left open – in an untidy state – after some types of failure. Use *CLOSE from the command line to close all open files.)

◆ the disc you are trying to use is corrupted

◆ the directory you are trying to use is full – a directory on a disc can hold up to 77 files or directories (the limit is different on a network)

◆ you have specified a disc drive number or filing system you don't have.

Click on OK to remove the dialogue box, and take appropriate action before you try to save the file again.

Closing documents

When you have finished working on a 1st Word Plus document, close it by clicking on the close icon at the top lefthand corner of the window. If you have made changes to the document since saving it, a dialogue box will appear asking if you want to save the changes first. If you click on Yes, the document remains on screen. This does NOT save the document; you still need to save the document explicitly with **File** from the Save sub-menu. If you click on No, the document will be closed and all the changes you have made since last saving the document will be lost.

When you have finished using 1st Word Plus, remove it from the icon bar using **Quit** in its icon bar menu. This frees the memory it occupied for you to use for another program. If you have any unsaved work – a document or supplementary dictionary – a warning dialogue box will appear for you to confirm that you really do want to quit and lose your unsaved work. If you are printing any files at the time you use **Quit**, printing will stop.

Keeping back-up copies

It is wise always to keep a back-up copy of your work. This will protect you against losing all your documents if your hard or floppy disc becomes corrupted, or you lose or destroy the floppy disc.

To make a back-up copy of your work, you need a formatted floppy disc. Use the icon bar menu from the floppy disc drive icon to format a disc using E format. When the disc is formatted, click on the floppy drive icon to display a directory display for the disc. You can now copy files and directories from your hard disc or another floppy disc into the directory display for the empty disc. If you are using just a single floppy disc drive, you will be prompted to switch the discs as necessary. The process for copying files and directories is described fully in the RISC OS *User Guide*, and in *Archimedes First Steps* (Dabs Press). A procedure for making a back-up copy of a floppy disc is described in chapter 1 of this book.

Label the disc that holds the back-up copies of your work and keep it safely. You should renew the back-up each time you make substantial changes to your files. You might want to make a fresh back-up every week, or even every day, as a routine. The frequency with which you should make back-up copies depends on how often you use the computer, but you should never leave it so long that you would lose a substantial amount of work if your working disc were to be lost or corrupted.

Documents containing pictures

When you import a picture into a document, 1st Word Plus keeps a reference to the picture's full pathname so that it can find the picture next time the document is opened. If you move or delete the picture, or save your document on a different disc, 1st Word Plus won't be able to find the picture and the document will be opened without the picture. The reference to the picture is deleted if you save the document without the picture, so it won't look for the picture next time you load it. However, if you close the document without saving it, you can copy the picture back into its original place in the directory structure and the document will be able to load the picture successfully again.

When you are saving a document with one or more pictures, you need to put it on the same disc as the pictures. When you make a back-up copy of the document follow these rules:

• If the picture and document are in the same directory, you can copy both into another directory or onto another disc (as long as they are both in the same directory again) and the document will still contain the picture.

• If the picture and document are in different directories, you can copy the document into another directory on the same disc and it will still contain the picture.

• If you move the picture into another directory or another disc, the document won't be able to find the picture.

• If you rename the picture, the document won't be able to find it.

Moving on...

The next chapter explains how to print a 1st Word Plus document.

15 Printing documents

Sooner or later, you will want to print your documents – there's little point in leaving your masterpiece on disc when you could have a large readership! When the time comes, you may find that you have to do battle with the 1st Word Plus printer driver generation procedure. If you are lucky, one of the printer drivers supplied will match the printer you have and all will be plain sailing. If you're unlucky, you'll have to write a printer driver of your own.

1st Word Plus doesn't use the standard Acorn printer drivers even though it's an Acorn product. Instead, it comes with a series of printer drivers intended to cover most dot-matrix printers – but just in case you have a printer that isn't catered for, there are also a couple of utilities to help you create your own printer drivers. You can't print 1st Word Plus documents on a PostScript laser printer except as plain text. Generating printer drivers is treated in Appendix 1: Coming to grips with printer drivers. This chapter tells you how to print a document assuming you already have a suitable printer driver.

Preparing to print

Before you can print a 1st Word Plus document, you need to have a suitable printer driver loaded. 1st Word Plus doesn't use the standard printer drivers that sit on the icon bar, but uses its own format of printer driver.

When you load 1st Word Plus, a printer driver is loaded automatically. As long as you haven't changed the default printer driver, this will be a driver for a 'Standard backspacing printer'. When you display the keypad window (using **Show keypad** in the 1st Word Plus icon bar menu), you will see this listed as the printer device:

The keypad window also shows that the printer is connected to the parallel port. This is the default setting: there is no check to make sure you really do have a printer connected to this port.

The computer has two 'ports' or places you can connect a printer. These are the serial port and the parallel port. 'Serial' and 'parallel' relate to the way in which the data from the computer are transmitted down the cable connecting it to the printer. They don't have to be used for different types of printer. You can have a printer attached to each if you want to. If there is already a printer attached to your computer, you can look at the back of the computer to see which port it is plugged into. It is most likely to be the parallel port.

If you are fitting a printer, look in the printer manual to see which port you should attach it to. If there is only one cable supplied with the printer, you will be able to tell from the plug on the end which port you need to plug it into, as the parallel and serial ports accept different types of plug. The manual might also use the terms Centronics interface for a parallel connection and RS423 for a serial connection. If you want to connect a printer with a serial interface to a BBC A3000, you will need to have a serial upgrade fitted to the computer. You can ask your dealer to do this for you. If your computer is connected to a network (in a school, for example), there may be no printer attached to your own computer. This doesn't mean you won't be able to print anything – there is probably a printer somewhere on the network and you should be able to use this. If you are using a network printer, there is said to be a printer on the network port even though this isn't really a physical port like the parallel and serial ports.

When you have decided which port to use for your printer, or found out which port a printer is attached to, you need to tell 1st Word Plus. If it is using the parallel port, you don't need to do anything, as this is selected by default anyway. If you are using the serial or network port, you need to click in the icon showing the port in use until the name of the one you want is shown. The ports are shown in sequence: parallel – serial - network. The sequence repeats, so you can go through it again if you miss the one you wanted.

A bit about printer drivers

A printer driver is a piece of software that tells the printer how to interpret the codes it is sent from the computer. When you send a 1st Word Plus file to the printer, the printer receives the text, and the codes that describe the special formatting and styling options you have used. These codes are peculiar to 1st Word Plus, and each printer has its own version of codes for the same operation. For example, an instruction to begin printing bold text will vary between printers and between computer programs. For this reason, printer drivers are necessary. They map the codes used by the program to the codes used by the printer, enabling the printer to translate the codes it receives into instructions it can understand.

If there isn't a 1st Word Plus printer driver supplied for your printer, or you use the one suggested and find that it doesn't work properly, you can create your own printer driver. The procedure is described in Appendix 1. You will need access to the manual for your printer, as this should list the codes the printer understands and the function of each.

Printer drivers supplied

1st Word Plus is supplied with twenty printer drivers intended to cover most standard printers, including dot-matrix and daisywheel printers. The printer drivers supplied are on the Utilities disc. They are:

ascii: A universal printer driver that prints just text, ignoring any special styling such as bold and italic.

standard: A printer driver to suit all types of printer, from a simple dot-matrix to a sophisticated laser-printer. The minimum requirement is that the printer has a backspacing function. It uses this to produce bold and underlining, but other special effects are not reproduced.

Daisywheel printers

brother: For Brother HR series daisywheel printers HR-15, HR-25 and HR-35 using a standard USA ASCII daisywheel. The HR-15 doesn't work very well using this printer driver with bold, justified text.

broth_uk: For Brother HR series daisywheel printers HR-15, HR-25 and HR-35 using a UK daisywheel. Again, the HR-15 doesn't work very well with bold, justified text.

daisy: A standard printer driver for daisywheel printers. If you are creating your own daisywheel printer driver, start with this one and customise it for your printer.

diablo: For Diablo and Diablo-compatible daisywheel printers using a standard USA ASCII daisywheel.

diabl_uk: For Diablo and Diablo-compatible daisywheel printers using a UK daisywheel.

juki: For the JUKI 6100 range of daisywheel printers using a standard USA ASCII daisywheel.

juki_uk: For the JUKI 6100 range of daisywheel printers using a UK daisywheel.

qume: For the Qume Sprint daisywheel printers, models 5, 9 and 11, using a standard USA ASCII daisywheel. For the Sprint 10, use the standard printer driver.

qume_uk: For the Qume Sprint daisywheel printers, models 5, 9 and 11, using a UK daisywheel. For the Sprint 10, use the standard printer driver.

9-pin dot-matrix printers

epson_fx: For Epson FX and Epson-compatible dot-matrix printers. However, some printers described as Epson-compatible are not really fully compatible and you might have problems with some effects. If you have an Epson FX-85 or FX-105, you will need to use the epson_lx driver instead.

epson_jx: For Epson JX colour dot-matrix printers and Epson EX dot-matrix printers fitted with the colour option. Light text is printed in red and colours in sprites are matched as closely as possible.

epson_lx: For Epson LX and Epson GX series printers, and the Epson FX-85 and FX-05 printers. These have a Near Letter Quality (NLQ) mode as an option, but not all 1st Word Plus effects can be printed in NLQ on these printers. 1st Word Plus will switch in and out of NLQ as necessary to give the best effect.

epson_rx: For Epson RX series printers.

ibm_grap: For the IBM Personal Graphics Printer.

ibm_prop: For the IBM Proprinter.

24-pin dot-matrix printers

epson_lq: For Epson LQ and SQ range printers. These have a full NLQ mode which supports all 1st Word Plus effects.

Laser printers

epson_gq: For the Epson laser printer.

RISC OS printer drivers

The standard RISC OS printer drivers weren't originally used for 1st Word Plus, but later versions of the RISC OS drivers will in fact print 1st Word Plus files.

You need to know the version number of your RISC OS printer driver to decide whether you should be able to print 1st Word Plus files with it. To find the version number, load the printer driver and then use **Info** on its icon bar menu to display a dialogue box like this:

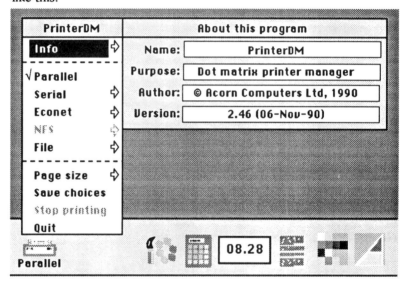

If the printer driver version number is 2.44 or later, you will be able to use it to print 1st Word Plus files, though you may find that some of the special effects don't work. If you have RISC OS version 3, the printer driver will probably be able to print bold, italic and underlined text, but footnotes may not be printed properly. It is always worth contacting your Acorn dealer to find out if you have the latest version of the printer drivers available; an updated version may offer better support for 1st Word Plus files.

If you want to be able to drag 1st Word Plus files to the printer driver icon to print them, you need to change a setting in the !Run file of 1st Word Plus. This is explained in the next chapter.

Loading a printer driver

If you don't want to use the standard printer driver, you will need to load another before you begin printing. To do this, open the directory 1WP_Print on the Utilities disc, and then the directory Config. This shows the printer drivers available:

Display the keypad window. Now drag the icon for the printer driver you want to use from the Utilities disc directory display to the keypad window. When you have done it successfully, the device icon on the keypad will show the name of the printer driver you have chosen.

If when you print out your document, you find that the printer driver doesn't work properly – it doesn't reproduce all the effects you expect – use the standard printer driver instead until you have the chance to write a new one specifically for your printer.

Changing the default printer driver

When 1st Word Plus starts up, it automatically loads a printer driver. This is always the printer driver called 1wp_print stored inside the 1st Word Plus application directory. To load a different printer driver when 1st Word Plus first starts up, you need to give another printer driver the name 1wp_print and put it in the application directory. Be sure you rename the original version first, so that you can reinstate it if you need to.

To rename the existing default printer driver, follow these steps:

1. Display a directory display showing the 1st Word Plus application icon. This will be on your working copy of the 1st Word Plus Program disc, or in your hard disc directory. If you are using 1st Word Plus on a network, get permission from the network manager before making any changes to 1st Word Plus defaults.

2. Hold down the Shift key and double-click on the !1stWord+ icon to open this directory display:

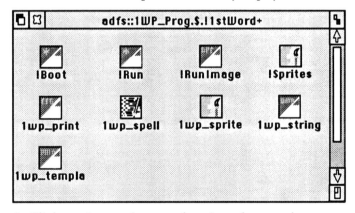

3. Click on 1wp_print to select it and press the menu (middle) mouse button. Using the **Rename** option, delete the name of this file and type a new name, then press Return.

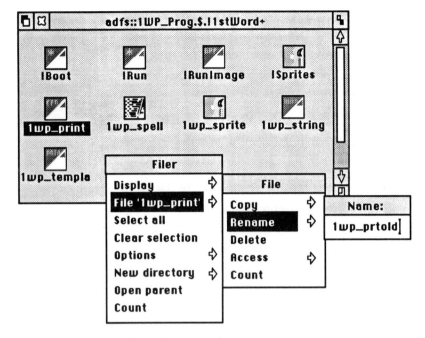

Don't close the directory display.

4. Open a directory display for the configuration file of the printer driver you want to use. This will probably be in the directory Config inside 1WP_Print on the 1st Word Plus Utilities disc, or in your hard disc or network directory. Drag the icon for the file you want to use into the viewer for the 1st Word Plus application directory. For example, if you want to use an Epson FX printer, drag the file epson_fx to the directory display. A copy of it will appear. Now use **Rename** again to name this copy 1wp_print. (Make sure you use the underscore character (_) and not the hyphen (-) or 1st Word Plus won't be able to find the printer driver. Underscore is on the same key as hyphen; use Shift to get it.)

5. Close the directory display. If you already have 1st Word Plus loaded, close it down using Quit on the 1st Word Plus icon bar menu and then

load it again. It will now use the new default printer driver. You can check by looking at the name in the device icon on the keypad window.

Don't change the default printer driver until you are sure the printer driver you are going to use instead works properly with your printer!

Printing a document

When you are ready to print a document, and you have loaded a printer driver, save your document. 1st Word Plus won't let you print a document that you are currently editing and which has unsaved changes.

Display the 1st Word Plus keypad window, and a directory display for the directory holding your document. Now drag the file icon for the document onto the printer icon on the keypad window. This dialogue box appears for you to make settings:

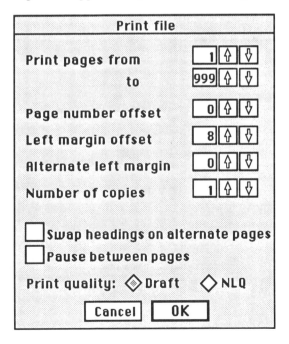

To alter any of the number settings, you can either

place the cursor in the writable icon, and delete the text there and then type the value you want, or you can click on the arrow icons to the right to increase or decrease the value.

Unless you alter the page range setting, all pages will be printed.

The **Page number offset** is the number that will be added to page numbers when they are calculated. When the page number offset is set to zero, pages will be numbered from one. This facility allows you to print chapters of a book with the page numbering running through the book rather just the file. For example, if the first chapter you print ends at page 25, you could set the page number offset for the second chapter to 25, and this would begin printing at 25+1=26. If that chapter ended at 48, you would set the page number offset for the next chapter at 48 to begin printing at 49. The page number offset is not saved with the file; you have to set it each time you print a document. The default value is always zero.

The **Left margin offset** tells the printer how far from the edge of the page to begin printing. It is measured as a number of character spaces. If you set it to zero, printing will begin at the extreme lefthand edge of the paper (or as close as your printer will print to the edge of the page). If you are using fanfold paper, you will need to set a left margin offset to avoid the perforations down the edge of the paper. If you have a sheet feeder, this may need a left margin offset. If you have a laser printer, this will not be able to print right at the very edge of the paper; the left margin will be the sum of the printer's own margin and the value you give for the left margin offset.

The **Alternate left margin** allows you to set a different left margin for odd- and even-numbered pages. If you leave this set to zero, the same margin will be used for all pages. However, if you are going to photocopy your document double-sided, and perhaps put it in a binder, you will probably want different margins on the two sides of the page. This will allow you to have a large enough margin for punching holes at the inside of the page. On a righthand page (odd number) the large margin will need to be on the left, but on a lefthand page (even number) the large margin will need to be on the right. You can't explicitly set a righthand margin in 1st Word Plus, but as you have set the width of the ruler (and so of the line), adjusting the lefthand margin will have the effect of altering the righthand margin too, as it moves the text block across the page. If you want to know how many characters fit across your page, print out a document with a wide ruler with the left margin offset set to zero and count the number of characters that print on a line. There is a suitable file on the disc that accompanies this book, called 'widefile'.

If you are going to want more than one copy of your document, you have the option of specifying the number of copies to print. It is slightly quicker to print several copies together by setting a value in this dialogue box than to print a single copy repeatedly.

If you have set a header and/or footer, you can choose to have the left/right position of these switched on alternate pages. This makes a difference only if you have used left and right elements; a centred header or footer will appear the same on both left and right pages unless you have very different left and right margins.

If you are using single sheets of paper and don't have a sheet feeder on your printer, you will probably want to instruct the printer to **Pause between pages**. This will give you the chance to put in a new sheet of paper. Click in the icon beside this option to place a star in it. When you send a document to the printer, a dialogue box will appear showing the status of the print run. It will show when the printer has paused for you to put in a new sheet of paper. When you have replaced the paper, click on Restart and the next page will be printed. If you click on OK, the dialogue box will disappear, but printing won't start again. If you click on Stop, the print run will be aborted. If you have clicked on OK, but want to restart the printer, click on the printer icon on the keypad window to redisplay the dialogue box. You can now click on Restart (or Stop).

If you have a dot-matrix printer which offers Near Letter Quality mode as an option, you can select this or the default draft mode. Choosing NLQ has no effect if you have a laser printer, daisywheel printer, or a dot-matrix printer that doesn't offer Near Letter Quality mode. Near Letter Quality mode gives a better printed image. It is achieved by printing twice as many dots to make up each letter, using an offset so that the second set of dots appears between the first set; this increases the density of ink on the page and makes the letters look more solid. It takes longer to print than standard (draft) mode.

Print status		
File	ADFS::19_00_Mon.$.TextA11	
Printer	Epson FH (9-pin matrix)	
Copies	1	Printing
Page	1	OK Pause Stop

When you click on OK, the file is sent to the printer. The label Status below the printer icon on the keypad window changes to Printing. If you click on this icon, the dialogue box illustrated above is displayed showing the status of the print run. If the printer is printing, you can click on Pause to stop it temporarily, or on Stop to abort the print run.

Depending on the printer you are using, you might find that short files or only a few pages print so quickly that you don't really have time to stop or pause them. You can use the **Pause between pages** option to force a pause if you want to be able to check the quality of the printing before proceeding, but remember that the file will then pause at every page break and wait for you to click on Restart.

Using the RISC OS printer drivers

If you have version 2.44 or later of one of the RISC OS printer drivers, you will be able to print 1st Word Plus, perhaps with some of its special effects, using the RISC OS printer driver rather than loading a 1st Word Plus printer driver. Using the RISC OS printer driver PrinterPS is the only way you can print 1st Word Plus files on a PostScript laser printer.

If you have not already displayed a directory display for 1st Word Plus or loaded 1st Word Plus, you can drag a 1st Word Plus file icon to the printer driver icon on the icon bar and a dialogue box will appear asking whether you want to print the text as 'plain', 'fancy' or not at all. Select 'fancy', which will reproduce as many of the styling features as possible, but not graphics. The degree of styling you will get will depend on the capabilities of your printer. 'Plain' does not give you just unstyled text, but prints control codes wherever they appear and the code [1e] in place of spaces; it's the same as if you printed a 1st Word Plus document from Edit.

Moving on...

The next chapter explains how to change some settings in 1st Word Plus to customise it to suit your own preferences.

16 Customising 1st Word Plus

There are a few options you can alter to tailor 1st Word Plus to your own requirements.

These are:

◆ setting 1st Word Plus to load or not load ASCII text (Edit) files

◆ setting 1st Word Plus to show or not show a warning before overwriting an existing document with the same name when you use **Save**

◆ print 1st Word Plus files from the RISC OS printer drivers (if you have a suitable version of the printer drivers).

Loading text files

By default, 1st Word Plus will load a plain text file (one with an Edit file icon) if you double-click on its icon in a directory viewer. If you have already displayed a directory display for 1st Word Plus, or have 1st Word Plus loaded, it will load a text file you double-click on (loading 1st Word Plus too if necessary), even if you also have Edit loaded. (If you are using RISC OS 3, you can hold down Shift and double-click on any type of file to load it as text, and it will be taken by 1st Word Plus in this way.) You can change this if you like, so that text files are loaded into Edit by default, and only 1st Word Plus documents are loaded into 1st Word Plus.

To set 1st Word Plus so that it doesn't automatically load text files, you need to edit the !Run file kept within the 1st Word Plus directory. Load 1st Word Plus or Edit so that you can edit the file. Display a directory display for the 1st Word Plus application directory, then hold down the Shift key and double-click on the !1stWord+ icon in the directory display to open the application directory. There will be a file called !Run which has a command file icon. Drag this icon to Edit or 1st Word Plus on the icon bar. It will open as a text file. Move the cursor to the line which reads:

```
Set FirstWordPlus$LoadTextFiles Yes
```

Delete Yes and type No, so that the line reads:

```
Set FirstWordPlus$LoadTextFiles No
```

Save the file. If you want to keep a copy of the original !Run file so that you can reset the default actions easily, make a copy of it or rename it before you save the new version of the file.

Reset your computer using the Reset button. When you load 1st Word Plus again, it will use the new setting and won't automatically load text files. As long as you have loaded Edit or opened a directory display for a directory containing Edit, Edit will load and open the text file when you double-click on the file icon.

Overwriting existing files

By default, 1st Word Plus displays a warning dialogue box asking you to confirm the action if you try to save a 1st Word Plus document with the same name as an existing 1st Word Plus file. The existing file will only be overwritten if you click on OK. If you routinely edit your files and save them again with the same name, you can turn off this warning, so that the default action is to save the file with whatever name you give it regardless of whether this will involve overwriting an existing file. To make this setting you need to change a line in the !Run file.

Open the !Run file in the way described above, and move the cursor to the line which reads:

```
Set FirstWordPlus$ForceOverwrite No
```

Delete the word No and type Yes so that the line reads:

```
Set FirstWordPlus$ForceOverwrite Yes
```

Now save the file as !Run again. You can make a copy of !Run or rename it before you save this version if you want to keep a copy of the default settings. Reset your machine. When you load 1st Word Plus in the future it will use the new setting and won't display the warning dialogue box.

Printing with the RISC OS drivers

If you have version 2.44 or later of the RISC OS printer drivers, you will be able to print 1st Word Plus text files without loading 1st Word Plus. By default, if you do not have 1st Word Plus loaded, but have displayed a directory display for a directory containing it, and you drag a file icon to the printer, 1st Word Plus will load (prompting you to insert the discs if necessary). The usual print dialogue box will then appear for you to set printing options. However, you can change a line in the !Run file to prevent this happening. You will then be able to drag 1st Word Plus document files to the printer icon on the icon bar and get the option of printing the file as plain text, as 'fancy' text or of cancelling the operation.

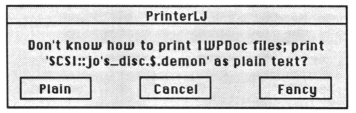

Choose 'fancy'; how many of the styling effects print properly will depend on the capabilities of your printer.

If you have a daisywheel printer, you can't do this as the standard RISC OS printer drivers don't support daisywheel printers.

To change the !Run file, open it as described above and move the cursor to the line which reads:

```
Set Alias$@PrintType_AF8 Run <Obey$Dir>.!Run %%*0 -print
```

Put the cursor at the start of the line and insert a vertical bar (I) so that the line reads:

```
|Set Alias$@PrintType_AF8 Run <Obey$Dir>.!Run %%*0 -print
```

This turns the line from an instruction to the computer into a comment. It will then have no effect. If you want to change it back at any point, just delete the vertical bar character. Save the file with the name !Run, first renaming the original version if you want to keep a copy of it.

Moving on...

The next chapter gives you some useful information on getting the best performance from 1st Word Plus.

17 Getting the most from 1st Word Plus

There are a few things you can do to make 1st Word Plus run better on your computer. This chapter explains how to make the most of the possibilities.

Memory

1st Word Plus uses at least 416K of RAM. If you don't have this much available, you won't be able to start it up. However, it may take more memory than this if it is available on your machine. 1st Word Plus will take the memory available in the Next slot. This is a slice of memory that is allocated for use by the next application that you load. Some applications take just what they need, and some take all that is available. 1st Word Plus is one of the greedy ones.

Here things get a bit complicated. There have been two releases of 1st Word Plus version 2. The first release version takes all the memory available in the Next slot, which by default is 640K. People using 1st Word Plus on a 1Mb machine complained that 1st Word Plus was taking all their available memory unnecessarily and that they couldn't run anything else at the same time if they loaded 1st Word Plus first. Acorn then released a second version, with 1st Word Plus limited so that it would take less memory and leave some for other things. If you aren't experiencing any problems, don't worry about it. If you are finding that 1st Word Plus is taking all the available memory on your machine and you can't do anything else at the same time, there are two ways you can check whether you have the hungry or the moderate version. You can look at the !Run file inside the !1stWord+ application directory, or you can find out using the Task Manager how much memory 1st Word Plus is taking. The first is quickest:

1. Open a directory display for the !1stWord+ application. Hold down the Shift key and double-click on the !1stWord+ icon to open the application directory.

2. Drag the icon for the file called !Run into Edit or 1st Word Plus so that you can look at it. Move to the end of the file, where there will be a line like this:

```
WimpSlot -min 416k
```

If the line is exactly like this, you have the earlier, hungry version; if it also has a -max value, you have the later version. You can reduce the maximum value (if there is one) to save extra memory.

3 Edit the line so that it says:

```
WimpSlot -min 416k -max 512k
```

4 Save the file. (You can make a copy of the original first if you are worried.)

5 Quit 1st Word Plus and then load it again. It should now take only a maximum of 512k, not all the memory available in the Next slot. To check how much it has taken, move the pointer over the system icon at the extreme right of the icon bar and press the middle button to display the menu. Click on Task display to open a window showing how the computer is using its memory.

There will be a bar for each application you have loaded, including 1st Word Plus. It should have taken only 512k.

You can set the -max value larger if you like, but this won't increase the speed at which 1st Word Plus operates. It will allow you to process larger files, but unless you want to work on very long documents or lots of pictures you won't need to increase it above 512k. With 512k, there will be about 255k available for your document (as long as you don't load the spelling checker). An average single-spaced page takes about 2k, so you can process a document up to about 120 pages long. (It's not a good idea to use every last scrap of memory available, and 1st Word Plus will warn you to save your document soon if you try to do so.) If you want to open multiple documents, more memory will be used up on just keeping the documents open, but there is this much space available for your work:

1 document	255k
2 documents	238k
3 documents	226k
4 documents	210k

(These figures may not match exactly what you can get on your own computer as memory handling can vary, but they give you a rough idea.) If you load the spelling checker, this will take up about 143k, so there will be less memory available for your documents. If you use a lot of pictures, or very large pictures, this will also take up a lot of memory. If your computer has sufficient memory, you will be able to alter the -max setting again if you want to process large documents containing pictures and using the spelling checker if you want to. Do this if 1st Word Plus displays a warning that it is running out of memory. (Close your file first, then reset the machine and reload afterwards 1st Word Plus).

You can save a little extra memory if you do want to use the spelling checker by loading it from the menu on the keypad window before you load your document. Doing this helps to prevent fragmenting the memory that is available; if you can leave the remaining memory in fair-sized chunks, you will be able to use it to process large documents.

Processing speed

The 1st Word Plus document window will redraw more quickly if you do not display graphics. If you are using pictures, turn graphics mode off to save memory.

1st Word Plus runs more quickly if you use a simple screen mode. You have to balance this against the quality of the display, though. When you are processing text, there is no point in using a very basic screen mode in which the text is difficult to see just to increase the processing speed. However, it is worth remembering that mode 12 is quicker than mode 15 and, on multisync monitors, mode 27 is fine, but mode 28 is slow. If you have a multisync monitor and can use mode 31 (which depends on the version of RISC OS you are using), this is better than 27 as it doesn't crop off the edge of the keypad window.

Palette

If you change the palette, and change the colour used to display text (colour 4 in a 16-colour mode), remember that bold text will still be shown in black. This is quite easy to see when the rest of the text is grey, but can be more difficult to spot if you set the text to a different colour. Light text will still be shown in light grey (or whatever you have changed colour number 2 to) – it won't be in a lighter version of the text colour you have set.

It can be helpful to set the light text to a different colour, especially if you are using 1st Mail a lot, but remember that all other instances of colour 2 on the desktop will also change. You can't change the colour of bold text without changing everything else, as redefining black affects all the shades of grey used on the desktop, too.

Moving on...

The next chapter gives you some hints and tips on using 1st Word Plus with other applications you might have.

18 Using 1st Word Plus with other programs

You can use 1st Word Plus to prepare text that you want to use in desktop publishing programs or in !Draw. This chapter explains how to prepare documents for use with:

◆ Acorn Desktop Publisher

◆ Impression

◆ Ovation

◆ Draw

You can also use text you have prepared with other systems with 1st Word Plus.

This chapter explains how to use text from View and Edit with 1st Word Plus.

1st Word Plus and Acorn Desktop Publisher

If you are going to prepare text for use with Acorn Desktop Publisher, you can save time by adding text styling and paragraph styles in 1st Word Plus.

Acorn Desktop Publisher will retain any of these text styles you have added to text in 1st Word Plus:

- bold

- italic

- underline

- superscript

- subscript.

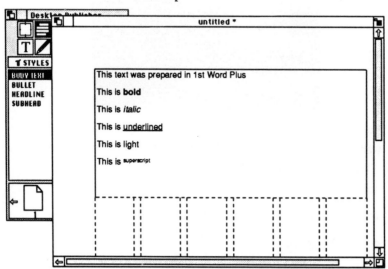

You can also set the paragraph styles of text blocks by giving the paragraph style name in angle brackets at the start of the paragraph. For example, the line

```
<headline>Forest News
```

in a 1st Word Plus document will be converted to 'Forest News' displayed in the headline paragraph style in Acorn Desktop Publisher. You don't need to specify paragraphs which are to be in body text, as any unmarked paragraphs will be given that style anyway.

You can use paragraph styles that don't exist in the style sheet you are going to use and they will be automatically created when you import the 1st Word Plus document. The styles will be the same as body text and you will have to use **Edit style** to give them different attributes, but their names will appear in the list of paragraph styles. The advantage of doing this is that you can tag all your headings, sub-headings and so on and when you define the attributes for the new styles in Acorn Desktop Publisher, the tagged paragraphs will all be converted to the right font and size immediately – you don't have to go through the document changing each paragraph to the style you want to use. This saves a lot of time that would otherwise be wasted on screen redraws as well as saving you the effort of finding and clicking on all the paragraphs you want to change.

Some things won't be retained by Acorn Desktop Publisher when you import a 1st Word Plus file. These are:

♦ automatic hyphens, which will be removed (sensibly, as the word probably won't come at a line end any more)

♦ tabs and multiple spaces, which will be converted to single spaces

♦ multiple returns, which will be converted to single returns (so blank lines you have inserted deliberately will be lost).

1st Word Plus and Impression

Impression (from Computer Concepts) can take in 1st Word Plus documents. If you want to prepare documents for use with Impression, you will need to install and use the appropriate Impression Loader Module, Load1WP. To load the module, double-click on its icon in a directory display. You will then be able to drag 1st Word Plus icons into an Impression document window.

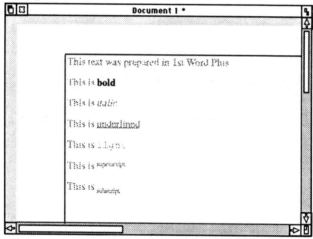

If you have a very early version of 1st Word Plus, this might not work properly. A 1st Word Plus file should have the filetype AF8. If you have difficulty loading a 1st Word Plus file into Impression, you need to change its filetype. Use **Display full info** to show information including the filetype in the directory display. If the type is not AFS, you can change it. If you are using RISC OS 2, press F12 to go to the command line beneath the icon bar and type:

```
settype pathname AF8
```

For example, if your file is called Letter2 in a directory Letters on a disc in drive 0, type:

```
settype :0.$.Letters.Letter2 AF8
```

If you are using RISC OS 3, you can change the filetype from the desktop. Open a directory display for the file and choose **Set type** from the **File** *filename* submenu. Delete the filetype shown in the writable field and type AF8, then press the Return key.

1st Word Plus and Ovation

If you want to prepare documents in 1st Word Plus to lay out using Ovation, you will need to save them as plain text files. There is no point adding any special style effects such as bold or italic as these will be lost when you save the file as text. Even so, you will probably find it easier to write and edit your text in 1st Word Plus first than in Edit, or in Ovation. When you have typed your text, turn off **WP mode** (in the Edit sub-menu) before you save the 1st Word Plus document. The file will have a text (Edit) icon when you have saved it. You can then drag the file into a frame in an Ovation document.

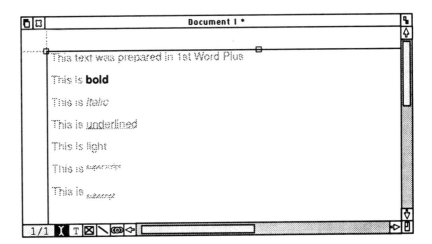

Draw

You can prepare text with 1st Word Plus to use in a Draw file, but you must save it as plain text (turning WP mode off). The file must end with a Return. Although you can't use 1st Word Plus to add styling to your text – it will be lost when you save the file as plain text – you can include any of the text formatting commands understood by Draw. These are listed and described in the RISC OS *User Guide*.

Using text prepared with other systems

You might sometimes want to use 1st Word Plus to work on text you have already prepared using another word-processing program or a text editor.

To use text prepared in Edit you need to convert it to a form 1st Word Plus can understand. 1st Word Plus uses special spaces, and begins with a special chunk of text that contains control codes giving instructions. When you start a 1st Word Plus document, you can't see these as they are just instructions to the program itself on setting up the ruler and so on, and they aren't displayed on screen. If you open a 1st Word Plus document in Edit, though, you will see them.

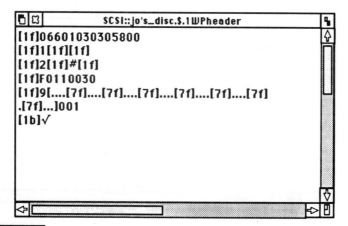

If you have an Edit document that you want to use in 1st Word Plus and you have the disc that accompanies this book, follow these steps:

1 Load your file into Edit and put the cursor at the top, before the first character.

2 Put the Examples disc that accompanies this book in the disc drive and open a directory display for it.

3 Drag the file 1WPHeader from the disc directory display into the Edit file so that the text appears before the text of your file.

4 Use **Find** in the Edit submenu to display the Find dialogue box. Type a space in the first field, and \x1e in the second field, then click on Magic characters to place a star in the icon, like this:

```
┌───────────────────────────────────────────┐
│               Find text                     │
│  ┌──┐┌────────┐┌─────┐                      │
│  │Go││Previous││Count│                      │
│  └──┘└────────┘└─────┘                      │
│         Find: ┌─────────────────────────┐   │
│               └─────────────────────────┘   │
│  Replace with:┌─────────\xle───────────┐   │
│               └─────────────────────────┘   │
│  ☐ Case sensitive:                          │
│  ☒ Magic characters:                        │
│                           \*=any string     │
│  \a=any letter or digit   \d=any digit      │
│  \.=any char \n=newline   \cX=ctl-X         │
│  \0=found string  \\=\     \xXX=hex char    │
└───────────────────────────────────────────┘
```

5 Click on Go. The found dialogue box appears:

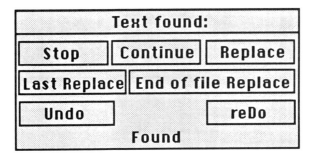

Click on **End of file Replace** to replace all spaces with the hexadecimal code [1e].

6 Save your file, giving it a new name if you want to keep your original Edit file.

7 Open your file in 1st Word Plus by dragging its icon onto the 1st Word Plus icon on the icon bar. The header text will not appear, and there will be a space for each [1e] code you could see in the Edit file. You will be able to use formatting and text styling commands, and you will be able to save your file as a 1st Word Plus document and open it again later in the usual way. When you use **Save File**, a 1st Word Plus document icon appears in the Save dialogue box.

You may sometimes want to use text you have prepared in View, or some other word-processing program, with 1st Word Plus. You will need to load the file into Edit and check the following:

• Does it have Returns where you would expect it to have them? If not, it probably has the code [0d] in place of Returns. Use **CR<=>LF** in the Edit submenu to change these.

• Does it have ordinary spaces? If so, change them to the code [1e] following instructions 4 and 5 above. If it has another code in place of spaces, change this to [1e]. For example, if it has [1c] at each space, swap this for [1e] by typing \x1c in the first field of the Find dialogue box and \x1e in the second field.

• Does it have any other codes of this type? If so, remove them by typing \x followed by the letters of the code (not the square brackets) in the first field and leaving the second field blank, then using **End of file** Replace when the first instance is found.

When your text is free of control codes like this, has [1e] for spaces and Returns in the right places, you can drag the 1st Word Plus header text into the file (put the cursor at the start first) and then carry on from instruction 6 above.

Moving on...

This completes part 1 of the book. The next part explains how to use 1st Mail, the mail merge program supplied with 1st Word Plus. You can use this to send out a batch of letters which are personalised but share large chunks of text.

Part 2

19 Using 1st Mail

Many people who buy 1st Word Plus never get around to using 1st Mail. This may be because they think they have no use for it, but it's often because they don't understand how to use it. This chapter explains what 1st Mail can do. Read it even if you don't think you need 1st Mail as you may be surprised to find that you could use it after all

What is 1st Mail?

1st Mail is a mail-merge program for use with 1st Word Plus documents. It works by merging information from two files: a 1st Word Plus document and a file of data, such as names and addresses. It produces a sequence of documents which share large chunks of text but are personalised. The irritating letters you probably receive telling you that you've won a Vauxhall Astra or a time-share in Benidorm are produced with a mail-merge program. The main text of the letter is included in all the copies that are sent out, but details of your name, address and perhaps the prize are pulled out of a file of data and inserted at strategic points in the letter.

How 1st Mail works

When you want to use 1st Mail, you need to create two documents. One is the *master document*, which contains the main text of the letter and some instructions to tell 1st Mail how to arrange the text and retrieve information to insert in it. The other is the *data file*, the list of names, addresses and other details that will be inserted in the letters. You can create both of these using 1st Word Plus. The master document must be saved as a 1st Word Plus document, but the data file must be a plain text (Edit) file. You can create the data file in 1st Word Plus, but you need to save it with WP mode set off. There is more information on creating and saving master documents and data files in the next two chapters.

A typical master document might look this:

And the data file to go with it could look like this:

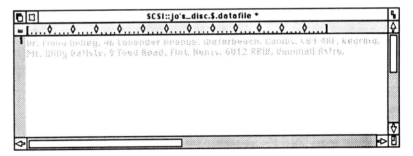

The first letter produced will look like this:

Dr Fiona Ridley
46 Lavender Avenue
Waterbeach
Cambs
Cb3 4RF

Dear Dr Fiona Ridley

We are delighted to be able to tell you that you, Dr Fiona Ridley,
have won a wonderful BRAND NEW

keyring!

To collect your keyring, just visit our showroom and listen to a
gruelling sales pitch about time-share cottages in Phnom Penh.
Your prize will be delivered to 46 Lavender Avenue the next day!

Hurry - you must reply within the next 5minutes!

Yours sincerely

Buster Weasel
Marketing Manager

This example is fairly simple; 1st Mail retrieves information from the data file and patches it into the appropriate places in the master document. It is possible to create complex sequences which instruct 1st Mail to go to a different file and read in a chunk of text, and then perhaps go on to yet another file to retrieve another chunk. But we'll look at straightforward uses of 1st Mail first.

Moving on...

The next chapter explains how to create a simple master document for use with 1st Mail.

20 Writing master document

The master document holds the main body of the text that will form the merged letters. It contains:

◆ the main text of the letter

◆ *commands*

◆ *keywords.*

Commands give 1st Word Plus a specific instruction, such as 'leave the righthand margin ragged' (the command for this is RAGGED).

Keywords are words you choose to identify the different pieces of information held in the data file. This chapter introduces master documents, but does not deal with all the commands. Some are described in the next two chapters because they relate to the way in which the data file is structured and interpreted, and the behaviour of 1st Mail when processing a merge job.

1st Mail commands

1st Mail recognises the following commands:

- chainfile
- clearscreen
- datafile
- display
- doubleline
- fieldsep
- includefile
- indent
- input
- justify
- margin
- noomit
- omitblank
- pagenum
- quotes
- ragged
- read
- recordsep
- repeat
- setval
- singleline
- skiprecord

Some of these you may never use, and you don't need to know about all of them to get started with 1st Mail. You need to be able to refer to a list of their names, though, as you can't use any command name as a keyword.

Keywords

A keyword is a name you give to an item in the data file. It appears in the master document, but is replaced by the appropriate piece of data when you produce the merged letters. For example, if your data file contains names and addresses, you will probably choose titles such as 'name', 'address1', 'address2' and so on for your keywords. Wherever you want an item to be retrieved from the data file and inserted into the letter, you need to give its keyword in light text in the master document. Typically, this will be names and addresses. In the example in the last chapter, it also includes the name of the prize. Keywords can be any words except the names of 1st Mail commands. They can't contain spaces.

Creating a simple master document

When you want to create a master document, begin by opening a new 1st Word Plus document and typing all the text that you want to appear in every copy of the document. Where you want to include something from the data file which will change from one copy of the letter to another (such as the recipient's name), use a keyword. You must use the same keyword for the same piece of information each time it comes up, so once you have decided to use 'name' as the keyword for a person's name, use this each time you want to repeat their name in the document. Type keywords in light type, or select the keyword after typing it and use **Light** in the Style sub-menu, or press F4 to change it to Light type.

Looking at the example again, you would start with a file like this:

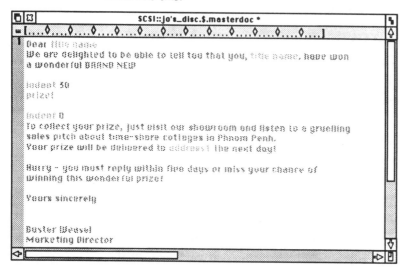

Each of the keywords will have to be matched to a piece of information in the data file. You need to tell 1st Mail to read in the these pieces of information and link them with the keywords. The instruction to do this, and some other instructions about general layout, come at the start of the master document, before the text begins.

The command you need to instruct 1st Mail to find the information for each keyword is READ. It must be followed by a list of all the keywords, in the order in which the corresponding information comes in the data file. This need not be the same order in which you use the keywords in the main body of the letter. The keywords must be separated by commas, but don't leave spaces between them. You do need a space after READ and before the first keyword in the list. It is a good idea to end the line with a comma, too. All 1st Mail commands must be in light type, at the start of the line. You can only use one command on a line. If there is any other information connected with a command – any parameters – this must be in normal type, not light type. In the case of READ, the keywords must be in normal type, even though elsewhere you would put keywords in light type. You can type the command and keywords in upper or lower case, it doesn't matter. So for our example, the read command would need the format:

```
read title,name,address1,address2, address3, postcode,prize,
```

Don't forget the light type for the command name. On screen, it looks like this:

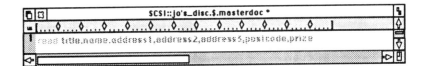

The READ command is the only command you have to include for the master document to work, though you must also use REPEAT if you want to generate more than just the first letter. There is a large number of other commands you can use to control the layout of the letters produced, and how 1st Mail uses the data file(s).

Printing several letters

When 1st Mail processes your master document, it will read to the end, switching data from the data file for the keywords, until it comes to the end of the document. It will then stop unless you instruct it to read the next set of data and print the next letter. To instruct it to carry on when it has got to the end of the master document the first time, you need to use the command REPEAT. Put this right at the

end of the letter and precede it by a hard page break
if you want to start each letter on a new page

Buster Weasel
Marketing Director
repeat

(described below).

The REPEAT command tells 1st Mail to read
through the letter again, taking the next set from
the data file. It will meet the REPEAT command
again, of course, and continue to repeat until it runs
out of information in the data file.

Using just REPEAT and READ you can use 1st
Mail to create merged documents with personalised
details, each printed on a separate sheet of paper.
However, there are several other commands you can
use to control the appearance of the letters
produced and to allow more sophisticated
processing.

Layout options

Although you can create merged documents with a
simple layout using just READ and REPEAT, you
can generate better-looking letters if you use some
of these layout options to control the appearance of
the final documents:

- double or single line spacing

- justified or ragged text

- indents

- a righthand margin

- leaving a space for a keyword with no
  corresponding information in the data file.

Normally, your letters will be printed in single line
spacing. If you want to use double line spacing, for

all or part of the document, you need to use the command DOUBLELINE. The text that comes after this command will be printed in double line spacing. This means that an extra carriage return will be inserted at the end of each line. If you want to return to single line spacing, use the command SINGLELINE. You won't need to use this command unless you have already used DOUBLELINE, as single line spacing is used automatically. To use either of these commands, like any others, type the command name at the start of a line and in light type. Don't type anything else on the line. A blank line won't be printed for a line that contains only a command. If you want a blank line

> doubleline
>
> To collect your prize, just visit our showroom and listen to a gruelling sales pitch about time-share cottages in Phnom Penh. Your prize will be delivered to [address] the next day!
> singleline
>
> Hurry – you must reply within five days or miss your chance of winning this wonderful prize!

as well, you have to add one with a Return.

To collect your keyring, just visit our showroom and listen to a gruelling sales pitch about time-share cottages in Phnom Penh. Your prize will be delivered to 46 Lavender Avenue the next day!

Hurry – you must reply within five days or miss your chance of winning this wonderful prize!

The section of letter shown above would be printed like this:

You can use justified text, or text left ragged at the righthand margin. 1st Mail reformats the paragraphs of the generated document to take account of the different lengths of the pieces of data imported from the data file. You can mix justified and unjustified text in the same document. The default is to use ragged text, so if you want this all through your document, you don't need to do anything. If you want the whole document to use justified text, add the command JUSTIFY at the top of the file, before the body text. If you want to use both ragged and justified text, use the command JUSTIFY to start justified text and RAGGED to finish it.

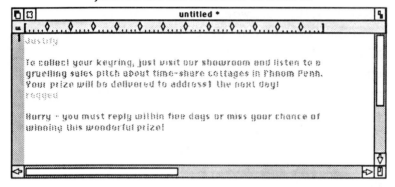

The section of letter shown above would be printed like this:

To collect your keyring, just visit our showroom and listen to a gruelling sales pitch about time-share cottages in Phnom Penh. Your prize will be delivered to 46 Lavender Avenue the next day!

Hurry - you must reply within five days or miss your chance of winning this wonderful prize!

You can control the lefthand margin by setting an indent. The INDENT command must be followed by a number showing how many characters you want to indent the text by. The number must not be in light type, even though the command must be. The indent you set will be used until you use another INDENT command. If you want to remove the indent, use INDENT 0. The name of the prize is indented in the example letter.

You can control the righthand margin using the MARGIN command. This must be followed by a number showing the size of the margin (counted in characters). Again, the number must not be in light type even though the command is. The margin you set will be used until you use another MARGIN command. To remove a margin, set it back to the width of the ruler. In our example, the ruler is 65 characters wide, so the command MARGIN 65 reverses the effect of MARGIN 20.

```
margin 20
To collect your prize, just visit our showroom and listen to a
gruelling sales pitch about time-share cottages in Phnom Penh.
Your prize will be delivered to address1 the next day!
margin
```

```
Hurry - you must reply within five days or miss your chance of
winning this wonderful prize!
```

The section of the letter shown above would be printed like this:

```
To collect your
keyring, just visit
our showroom and
listen to a gruelling
sales pitch about
time-share cottages in
Phnom Penh. Your prize
will be delivered to
46 Lavender Avenue the
next day!
```

```
Hurry - you must reply within five days or miss your chance of
winning this wonderful prize!
```

Finally, you can choose whether or not to leave a blank line if the information corresponding to the keyword used in the line is missing from the data file. For example, if you have keywords Address1, Address2, Address3, Postcode, and one of your correspondents has only a two line address, you won't have any data for Address3. You will need to make a blank entry in the data file (explained in the next chapter), and there will be nothing to substitute for the keyword Address3 in the master document. By default, 1st Mail will print a blank line if it encounters an empty data field in the data file, but you can instruct it not to using the command

OMITBLANK. This causes 1st Mail to omit the blank lines it would have inserted – rather a confusing way of handling the situation! If you want to reverse the effect later on in the letter, adding blank lines for future empty fields, use the command NOOMIT. This instructs 1st Mail not to omit the blank lines – ie, put blank lines in – when it encounters an empty data field. For example, if you had these keywords in the text in your master document:

address1

address2

address3

postcode

and your data file included a person with the address 12 Willborough Grove (address1), Bristol (address2) BR3 7HY (postcode) it would print as:

12 Willborough Grove
Bristol
BR3 7HY

If you used the command OMITBLANK before the address appeared in the letter, though, it would print as:

12 Willborough Grove
Bristol
BR3 7HY

which is probably what you would want.

Page breaks and letters

It is difficult to conceive of circumstances when you would not want to start each copy of a letter on a new page, yet 1st Mail doesn't do this automatically. If you want to start a new page for each letter, you need to put a hard page break at the end of the text. This must come before the REPEAT command.

You can include a page number in your merged letters by using the header and footer facilities in the usual way, putting a hash (#) character where you want the page number to appear. However, when you process the mail merge job, the pages printed will be numbered consecutively – each letter will not begin with page 1. For example, if you print three copies of a three page letter, the first will be numbered 1-3, the second 4-6 and the third 7-9. It's not very likely that this is what you would want. To restart the page number counter at 1 at the start of each new letter, you need to use the command PAGENUM 1 in the master document. This must appear before the text of the letter begins. The command must be in light type, but the 1 must be in normal type. You can restart the page counter at any number you like; PAGENUM 5 would start all letters with page 5, for example.

Moving on...

The next chapter explains how to write a data file for use with 1st Mail, and describes some additional commands you can use in the master document to control the way the data file is read.

21 Writing data files

The information to include in a merged letter is taken from a data file and substituted wherever a keyword appears in the master document. This chapter explains how to write a data file and how to use some commands in the master document that give you more flexibility when creating data files.

Data file structure

A data file must be a plain ASCII text (Edit) file. You can create it with 1st Word Plus, but must save it with WP mode set off.

The data file usually contains all the information that will be merged with the master document to create the letters. It is divided into *records* and *fields*. There is a record for each letter that will be created. The record holds data in several fields, one for each keyword used in the master document. The data file used in the example we have been looking at looks like this:

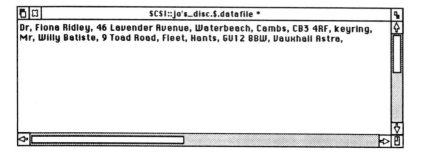

Each line is a separate record. The fields within each record are separated by commas. A record must be only one line long. This limits its length to the length of a line in Edit or 1st Word Plus: 160 characters.

If we compare one of the records with the READ command at the start of the master document, you can see how the information is mapped to the keywords so that it will be used in the right places in the final document. The first record is:

```
Dr,Fiona Ridley,46 Lavender Avenue, Waterbeach,Cambs,CB3 4RF,keyring,
```

The read command in the master document lists the keywords like this:

```
read title,name,address1,address2, address3,postcode,prize,
```

The keywords are mapped to fields in the data file in the order in which they appear. The first keyword, title, is mapped to the item in the first field, Dr. The second keyword, name, is mapped to the text in the second field, Fiona Ridley, and so on. It is useful to use keywords that show the type of information you intend to retrieve from the data file because then you can spot any mistakes easily. It also makes it easy to put the keywords and the fields in the right order in the READ command and the data file. However, 1st Mail doesn't look for a field of the right type, it just takes the next in sequence, so if you had listed the keywords in the READ command as name,title they would be mapped respectively to Dr and Fiona Ridley. When you printed the letter, you would find it was addressed to Fiona Ridley Dr.

The usual way to write a data file is to separate the fields with commas. You can then use spaces within the fields (as in the name Fiona Ridley) without confusion. By default, 1st Mail will accept spaces as ordinary characters, but will treat all commas as field separators. This means that if you gave the address as '46, Lavender Avenue' the two parts would be mapped to two different keywords, '46' being assigned to Address1 and ' Lavender Avenue' to Address2. The comma tells 1st Mail that the information for that keyword is finished, and it can go on to the next field and map that text to the next keyword. If you want to include a comma in the text you are substituting for a keyword, you need to enclose the text in quotation marks. If you want to use a lot of commas in the text, you can set different characters to be the field separators. These options are explained below, in the section *Setting field and record separators*. You must put a comma at the end of the record, too. This means that all lines in the data file must end with a comma.

The records are separated from each other by Returns. Each record begins on a new line. 1st Mail will read one record for each letter it is producing. However, if there are too many or too few fields in a record, 1st Mail will either stop short of the end of the record or take some fields from the next one, so if you don't have any information for one of the fields and want to leave it blank, put two commas next to each other (,,) to show there is a blank field. If we wanted to include a person with a two-line address in the data file in the example, the line to add could look like this:

```
Mrs,Beryl Carter,12 Willborough Grove, Bristol,,BR3 7HY,keyring
```

If you have not used the OMITBLANK command in the master document and have put an empty field in the data file, a blank line or space will be left in the letter in place of the keyword mapped to the empty field.

Using commas and quotation marks in data file text

If you want to use commas in text you are mapping to keywords, you can enclose the fields concerned in quotation marks. You can use single or double quotation marks for this. 1st Mail will take anything between two matching quotation marks as text that should be printed exactly as it appears, including commas. So whereas

```
46, Lavender Avenue,
```

would be mapped to two keywords,

```
'46, Lavender Avenue',
```

would be mapped to only one.

One consequence of this is that you can't use a single quotation mark (and therefore you can't use an apostrophe) on its own as 1st Mail will interpret it as the first of a pair. If you want to include an apostrophe, you need to enclose the field containing it in double quotation marks:

```
"St Peter's Drive",
```

Remember when you are using quotation marks to enclose a field that you need to put the comma separating this field from the next *after* the closing quotation mark.

Setting field and record separators

If you want to use a lot of commas in your data file text, you can nominate different characters to act as field separators. If you want to use a lot of quotation marks, you can nominate other characters to enclose text you want printed exactly as it appears in the data file. For example, if you like to print all your addresses with a comma after the house number, it will be inconvenient to have to put all the lines containing a house number inside quotation marks. You could choose a character you are not going to use in addresses, such as /, and use this as a field separator.

To set the character used as a field separator, you need to include the command FIELDSEP in the master document. You will need to include it in each master document that uses the same datafile, so if you are using / as a separator in your mailing list file, all of your master documents that use the mailing list will need the FIELDSEP command. The FIELDSEP command must be followed by a decimal number that identifies the character you want to use. This is not at all obvious. The nicest way to have done it would be to allow you just to type the character you want to use after FIELDSEP, but instead you have to look up the decimal number that identifies it. The 1st Word Plus manual doesn't list the numbers, and refers you to the RISC OS *User Guide*. All the characters you might want to use are listed in Appendix 2. For example, to use the character / as a separator, you would need to put the command FIELDSEP 47 in the master document. As usual, you need to type the command FIELDSEP in light type and the number in normal text.

You can set up to twenty field separators. To define more than one, list the numbers, separated by commas in a single FIELDSEP command. For example, FIELDSEP 47,42,124 sets the characters backslash (/), asterisk (*) and vertical bar (I) as field separators. By default, 1st Mail recognises comma (character 44) and tab (character 9) as field separators.

You can set record separators in a similar way, using the command RECORDSEP in the master document. By default, the characters recognised as record separators are Return (character 10) and formfeed (character 12). You can set up to twenty characters as record separators. For example, to set characters + and - as record separators you would need to include the command RECORDSEP 43,45 in the master document. You can't use the same characters as you have chosen as field separators, as 1st Mail won't be able to distinguish between the end of a field and the end of a record.

As mentioned earlier, if you want to use in your data file text a character you have chosen as a field or record separator, you need to enclose it in quotation marks. However, if you want to use both types of quotation marks (' and ") in the text of your data file, you will need to define different characters to act as quotation marks and use them to enclose text you want printed literally. For example, if you wanted to include the text Pete's "new" hat, you couldn't use either single or double quotation marks to enclose the text. To use a different character to enclose literal text, you need to use the command QUOTES in the master document, with the decimal number of the character you want to use. To set ! for enclosing literal text, you would need to put the command QUOTES 33 in the master document. You could then include as a field in the data file the text !Pete's "new" hat! and all the text between the two ! characters would be printed exactly as it appears.

Moving on...

The next chapter explains how to process a mail-merge job and describes some additional commands you can use in the master document to control some features of processing.

22 Processing a mail-merge job

This chapter explains how to process a mail-merge job and control the screen display while the merge is being processed. Before you can process a mail-merge job you need to load a printer driver. 1st Mail does not automatically use the same printer driver as 1st Word Plus.

Loading 1st Mail and a printer driver

You don't actually need to load 1st Mail until you want to process a mail-merge; you can generate master documents and data files from 1st Word Plus without 1st Mail loaded.

When you are ready to run a mail-merge, you need to load 1st Mail. Open a directory display for the directory containing 1st Mail (it is on the 1st Word Plus Program disc). Double-click on the !1stMail icon; 1st Mail loads, and its icon appears on the icon bar. It looks like this:

Next, you need to load a printer driver for 1st Mail. Move the pointer over the 1st Mail icon on the icon bar and press the middle mouse button to display the icon bar menu. Choose **Printer**; this dialogue box appears for you to set the printer driver and printer port:

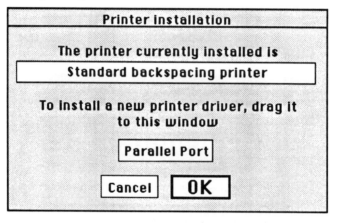

To load a printer driver, open a directory display for the printer driver you want to use and drag its icon to the dialogue box. The name of the printer driver you have loaded will appear in the top icon.

Check that the icon beneath shows the port that your printer is attached to. Click on this icon to show the options in rotation. You can have your printer connected to the parallel or serial port of your own computer, or linked to a network (in which case you should choose Network port). If you don't want to send your letters directly to the printer, you can send them to a file instead. It is a

good idea to do this at first when you begin using
1st Mail as it saves a lot of time and paper while you
experiment. The file produced is a standard 1st
Word Plus document, which you can then print
using the 1st Word Plus printer drivers from the
keypad window in the usual way. When you have
made the settings you want, click on OK.

Executing the mail-merge

When you have loaded a printer driver and saved
your master document and data file, you can process
the mail-merge job. Open directory displays to show
both the master document and data file. First, drag
the file icon of the master document to the 1st Mail
icon on the icon bar. The 1st Mail window will
open, along with a dialogue box for you to set
printing options.

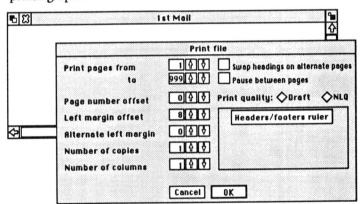

If you have chosen to print to a file, you won't get
the dialogue box showing printing options, just a
standard save file icon for you to give a name for the
file you are going to create. Name the file and drag
the icon to a directory display.

You can set the same printing options for a 1st Mail
job as for a 1st Word Plus document, with the
additional option to set the number of columns you
want to print on each page. If you alter this to a

number other than one, extra options appear in the area labelled **Headers/footers ruler** on the right:

```
┌─────────────────────────────────────────────────────────────────┐
│                           Print file                             │
│                                                                   │
│  Print pages from     [ 1][↑][↓]  [ ] Swap headings on alternate pages │
│              to       [999][↑][↓] [ ] Pause between pages        │
│                                                                   │
│  Page number offset   [ 0][↑][↓]  Print quality: ◇ Draft  ◇ NLQ  │
│                                                                   │
│  Left margin offset   [ 8][↑][↓]  ┌──────────────────────────┐   │
│  Alternate left margin [ 0][↑][↓] │  Headers/footers ruler   │   │
│  Number of copies     [ 1][↑][↓]  │  Length [65][↑][↓]       │   │
│  Number of columns    [ 2][↑][↓]  │  Pitch: ◇ Pica  ◇ Condensed │  │
│                                   │         ◇ Elite ◇ Expanded │   │
│                                   └──────────────────────────┘   │
│                                                                   │
│              [ Cancel ]   [  OK  ]                               │
└─────────────────────────────────────────────────────────────────┘
```

[1mailprhf]

This is described in the next chapter, More advanced use of 1st Mail.

When you have set the options you want to use, click on OK. A message will appear in the 1st Mail window telling you that the job has been started. It has the format:

`1ST MAIL filename started`

`DATA FILE`

At this point you need either to type the name of the data file you want to use, or drag its icon into the 1st Mail window. If the data file is in the same directory as the master document, you just need to type the file name. If it is in a different directory, you need to type the full path name. It is usually simpler to drag the file icon into the 1st Mail window, but you can't drag it if the file is in the same directory – you have to type the file name. When you have identified the data file, 1st Mail will process your mail-merge job. If you have used commands to control the screen display during processing, the screen will be cleared, or will display a message, as you have instructed (this is described below). When the mail-merge job has finished (if it has been successful), a message like this appears in the window:

```
1ST MAIL filename finished
```

Unfortunately, the job isn't always successful first time. You might not get any letters at all, and if you do they may not be what you expected. It is a good idea to send the letters to a file rather than directly to the printer the first time; this lets you sort out any problems without wasting lots of paper and time. The section after the next explains the causes of some problems you might have.

Controlling the screen display

If you want to be able to see how well the mail-merge process is doing, you can instruct 1st Mail to display a message on the screen, such as:

```
Processing your letter to name: please wait.
```

The message will be updated for each letter, so you will be able to see how far through the data file processing has got.

To display a message during processing, include the command DISPLAY in the master document. Put it before the letter text, but after the READ line. After DISPLAY in light type, put the message you want displayed in quotation marks. You can include keywords in the message – such as the name of the person the letter is addressed to – and these must be in light type. The rest of the message must be in normal type. In our example, the DISPLAY line is:

```
display "Producing letter to title name: please wait"
```

This displays a message such as:

```
Producing letter to Dr Fiona Ridley: please wait
```

in the 1st Mail window as the letters are processed. The name and title of each person is used in the message as their letter is processed. The messages will build up on the screen as more letters are processed. If you want to see just the current message, you can use the command CLEAR to remove the last message before the message for each letter is displayed. Include the CLEAR command in the master document, either immediately before the REPEAT command or at the top of the document, after the READ line but before the DISPLAY command. All you need to type is CLEAR in light type; there is no text to follow it. To clear the last message from the screen before displaying the next one, the example master document would have to be changed to look like this:

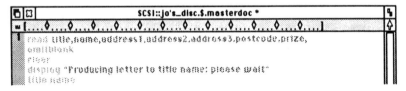

Problems with 1st Mail

If there is a problem with either your master document or data file, 1st Mail may do any of the following:

◆ not process the job at all, and display an error message in the window

◆ process the job, at least partially, and display an error message in the window

◆ process the job, display no message, but produce letters with the wrong format.

Unfortunately, 1st Mail error messages are not usually very helpful and it may take a while to work out what exactly has gone wrong.

If nothing is printed, or only part of the first letter, you may see this error message:

```
ERROR: Keyword not found [word] on
line [no] of [masterdoc]1ST MAIL
[masterdoc] aborted
```

This happens if:

◆ you have used a keyword in the text which isn't listed in the READ line

◆ you haven't put any keywords in the READ line

◆ you haven't included a READ line, but have used keywords.

(In the last case, 1st Mail won't prompt you for a data file before starting the attempt to process your master document.)

Open your master document and correct the READ line.

If something is printed, you may see this message:

```
Unexpected end of data file on line
[no] of [masterdoc]1ST MAIL
[masterdoc] aborted
```

You may also find that the first letter has been printed correctly but thereafter a space is substituted for the first keyword in the text and the others are then used out of sequence. This message usually appears if there are too many or too few records. Check that you have the right number of records in each line of the data file. There must be a record, or a comma to indicate a blank field, for each keyword listed in the READ line. If each line does have the right number of records, make sure there is a comma after the last keyword in the READ line.

If the letters print, but the keywords are used in the wrong places, you won't necessarily get any error message at all. If there is no message, it is likely that you have missed out a separator somewhere. This type of error is characterised by printout like this:

```
Dear CB1 3DR
Thank you for your letter of 23,
Princess Way...
```

Other errors will be fairly easy to diagnose. For example, if you wanted double-spaced text but it has come out single spaced, either you didn't include the DOUBLESPACE command or you forgot to put it in light text (in which case it will be printed as part of the letter text). If one letter starts straight after another on the same page, you haven't put a hard page break before the REPEAT command. However, if there are problems with the page length or margins, these are not specifically 1st Mail difficulties. You have either set the wrong page length for the paper you are using (set with the **Page layout** dialogue box from the 1st Word Plus Page menu) or the printer settings are incorrect.

Moving on...

The next chapter explains how to use some of the more sophisticated facilities of 1st Mail. These allow you to switch between files as a job is executed, and plan complex sequences of file execution. Although these don't sound very useful if you are planning fairly straightforward mailshots, they have more applications than you might imagine. You can also use 1st Mail to print multi-column text, which is useful for address labels.

23 More advanced use of 1st Mail

This chapter explains how to use the more sophisticated facilities offered by 1st Mail. They can be useful, even if initially you think they are too complex for what you require. This chapter explains how to:

◆ substitute large chunks of text in a mail-merged document

◆ use command files to process several mail-merge jobs

◆ print multi-column text (which is useful for address labels).

Inserting larger chunks of text

When you use 1st Mail with the commands we have
looked at so far, processing is a matter of simple
substitution of information in one file for keywords
in another. 1st Mail reads the master document,
goes to the data file for the records in the first field
to substitute for the keywords and generate the first
letter, then goes through the master document
again, going back to the data file for the records in
the second field to generate the second letter, and so
on.

The substitutions you can make are limited to a
single line in a text file, a maximum of 160
characters, for each letter. This can be quite limiting,
so a couple of other methods are provided which
allow you to include longer chunks of text in a
letter.

The command INCLUDEFILE, followed by a file
name, instructs 1st Mail to retrieve the text from
another file and include it in the text of a letter. For
example, if you have two scales of charges which you
apply to different customers (unethical, but never
mind), you might have a master document like this
for one batch of letters:

```
...we will be happy to quote for the job. Our scale of charges is
shown below.

includefile cheap

I look forward to hearing from you in the future.
```

Another batch of letters might use the other scale:

```
...we will be happy to quote for the job. Our scale of charges is
shown below.

includefile expensive

I look forward to hearing from you in the future.
```

If you want to include a different chunk of text in each letter, you need to write and save each as a separate file. You also need to use the INCLUDEFILE command interactively. This means that instead of typing a filename in the master document, leave INCLUDEFILE on a line on its own. 1st Mail will then prompt for a file name at the appropriate point of processing each letter. For example, if you are writing letters to all your relatives updating them on your life, you might want to tell different people different things. If you use INCLUDE FILE without a file name, you can include different chunks of text as appropriate. Your letter might be like this:

Dear name

Just a note to let you know how i'm getting on and to thank you for the present you sent for my birthday.

includefile

I have also bought another dog...

When the master document is processed, a prompt will appear asking for the name of the file to include at this point:

```
Producing letter to Aunt Bettie:
please wait

  INCLUDE FILE
```

Type the name of the file you want to take the text from, and processing will continue. For example:

```
INCLUDE FILE Holiday
```

or

```
INCLUDE FILE Wedding
```

The first option, Holiday, would include the text from a file called holiday, perhaps producing a letter like this:

Dear Aunt Bettie

Just a note to let you know how I'm getting on and to thank you for the jersey you sent for my birthday.

I'm going to Thailand with Jack for a couple of weeks in March. It should be really good. We've got cheap flights, and I'm told it's very cheap to stay in quite good hotels, as long as you avoid the real tourist traps. Uncle Jim told me you have been to Thailand. I must give you a ring and we can chat about it before I go.I have also bought another dog...

The second option would include text from the file called Wedding:

Dear Granny

Just a note to let you know how I'm getting on and to thank you for the record token you sent for my birthday.

I went to Julie's wedding last week and expected to see you there. I hope you weren't ill. It was a lovely day and she looked super. Lots of people asked when I was going to get married – don't ask, I'm not going to.

I have also bought another dog...

There is an example of a master document and three files to use at the INCLUDE FILE prompt on the example disc that accompanies this book. They are in the directory Include. Drag the file Letter to the 1st Mail icon on the icon bar, and type the name 'data' when asked for the name of the data file. Include one of the files Carcrash, Holiday or Wedding for each of the letters as they are processed.

The text in a file used with INCLUDEFILE may contain 1st Mail commands. It is best not to use keywords, as the data for the keywords will be taken from the same data file as you are using for the master document. This means that unless all the files you use with INCLUDEFILE have the same number of keywords, and you make allowance for them when you write the data file, the substitution of data for keywords in the master document will get out of sequence.

When 1st Mail has finished processing the text in the included file, it returns to the master document and processes the remainder of that. In the examples above, you can see that the text of the letter continues after the included file, and all commands and keywords in the master document after the included text will be processed as usual.

If you want to stop processing the master document and go to another file, not returning to the master document at its end, use CHAINFILE instead. 1st Mail will process the master document until it meets the CHAINFILE command and then process the file named, but will not return to the master document afterwards. This is of limited use on its own, since if 1st Mail doesn't return to the original file, it can't process a REPEAT command and consequently you can only process one letter at a time. However, you can use CHAINFILE, as an instruction in a file called up with INCLUDEFILE, and processing will then return to the master document which contained the INCLUDEFILE command.

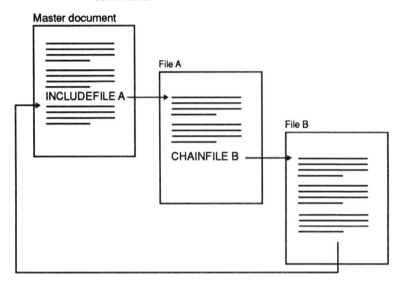

In this case, 1st Mail treats the text called in with CHAINFILE as additional material in the included file and behaves as though the chainfile text were present in the included file. This is easiest to understand if we look at an example.

In the letter to Aunt Bettie and Granny above, we have included some text that describes a wedding. If you wanted to tell several relatives about the wedding, but give more details to some than to others, could use CHAINFILE at the end of the file Wedding:

I went to Julie's wedding last week and expected to see you there. I hope you weren't ill. It was a lovely day and she looked super. Lots of people asked when I was going to get married – don't ask, I'm not going to.

chainfile

When 1st Mail has finished processing the text in Wedding, it will issue a prompt for you to type in the name of the file for the CHAINFILE command:

```
Producing letter to Aunt Bettie:
please wait INCLUDE FILE holiday
```

Producing letter to Granny: please wait
INCLUDE FILE wedding
CHAIN FILE

If there was an extra file called Details, this would be included after the text from the file Wedding, and 1st Mail would then return to the master document and continue processing that. The letter would look like this:

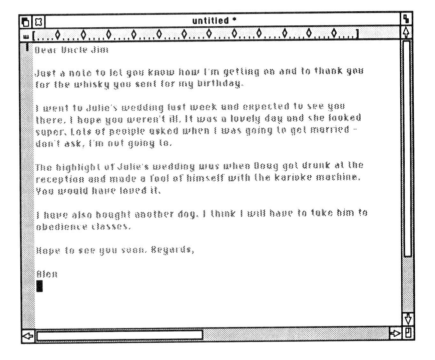

As with INCLUDEFILE, you can use CHAINFILE with a file name or without. If you use it without a file name, a prompt will appear in the 1st Mail window when 1st Mail meets the CHAINFILE command. Type the name of the file you want to use. If it is in the same directory as the letter you are processing, you only need to give the name of the file; if it is in a different directory, you need to give the full pathname or drag the file icon into the 1st Mail window. (You can't drag the icon into the window if the file is in the same directory as the letter you are processing; if you try, you will get the error message ERROR: Unable to open file.)

Using command files

If you use 1st Mail a lot, you can use command files to simplify your mail merges. You can process several master documents, all using the same data file, and you can supply a value for one or more keywords that will be used throughout the run.

A command file is a 1st Word Plus file. It uses commands in light text, just like a 1st Mail master document. Here is an example:

```
datafile data
setval today, "23 February"
includefile letter
```

```
datafile datasetval today, "23 February"includefile letter
```

This is a very simple command file. It instructs 1st Mail to:

- use the file called data to supply the data that will be exchanged for keywords

- use the text '23 February' whenever it encounters the keyword 'today' (SETVAL sets a value for one of the keywords in the master document.)

- process the master document called 'Letter'.

If you were using a command file like this, you would need to change the date in the second line each day you used it. You can avoid this by using an interactive command, INPUT, instead:

```
datafile date
setval "What is today's date? ",today
includefile letter
```

Now the second line will prompt for the date when the command file is run. The prompt shown enclosed in quotation marks will appear in the 1st Mail window, and the text you type in response to the prompt will be linked to the keyword 'today'. When you are writing a command file, remember to leave a space after the text of the prompt and before the closing quotation mark. If you don't, the text you type in response to the prompt when you run the command file will come directly after the prompt, it won't be separated from it by a space. This doesn't affect the way the command file works, but it looks a bit confusing and untidy on the screen.

The 1st Word Plus program disc supplies an example of a command file like this, but as the sample letter doesn't actually use the keyword 'todaydate' that it prompts for, it isn't obvious what is happening.

Imagine you are going to use the simple command file shown above with a file called Letter which starts like this:

```
read name,address1,address2,address3,postcode
omitblank

name
address1
address
address
postcode

today

Dear name

I am pleased to be able to tell you...
```

1st Mail will look for a datafile called Data to find the information to substitute for the keywords name, address1, address2, address3 and postcode. It will display the prompt 'Date? ', and whatever you type in response to the prompt will be used in the letter wherever the keyword 'today' appears. Because the command file tells 1st Mail to use the master document Letter, it will begin processing this without you having to specify the name of the file you want to use as a master document. If you give the name of a file that is not in the same directory as the command file, you need to give its full pathname. You can use INCLUDEFILE without a file name, in which case a prompt will appear when you process the command file asking for the name of the master document you want to use.

To write a command file, open a new 1st Word Plus document, and type in the commands and the text that goes with them as usual. The commands and keywords must be in light type, as in a 1st Mail master document. You can only use one command on each line. Any text that is going to appear on the screen as a prompt must be enclosed in quotation marks. Use the command INPUT to retrieve text interactively by displaying a prompt on screen. After the prompt, put a comma and then the name of the keyword the information is to be mapped to. Don't put a space after the comma. The format of the line should be:

```
input "What is today's date? ",today
```

When you have finished, save the command file as an ordinary 1st Word Plus document.

To run a command file, drag its icon to the 1st Mail icon on the icon bar, or into the 1st Mail window. Any prompts will appear in the 1st Mail window. The letters will be sent to the printer or a file, using the output option you have set with the 1st Mail icon bar menu option **Printer.**

The very simple command file we have looked at so far would not really be worth using. Command files are particularly powerful in that they enable you to process a batch of mail-merge jobs in sequence, inserting any extra information you need by giving data for keywords interactively. Suppose you had to send a mailshot to all the companies on your office's mailing list, regularly. You would always use the same data file, Maillist, but would send different letters. You might use a command file like this to make things easier:

```
datafile maillist
input "What is the date? ",date
input "What is the subject,matter? ",subject
input "What are you enclosing with the letter? ",enclose
input "What is the name of the letter file? ",filename
include filename
```

The first line tells 1st Mail to use the mailing list file to retrieve data. This will provide the names and addresses.

The second line displays a prompt, ie 'What is the date?' , on screen. Whatever you type in response will be used each time 1st Mail meets the keyword in the master document.

The third line displays a prompt asking for the subject matter. Again, the response will be used each time the keyword 'subject' appears in the master document.

The fourth line displays another prompt, this time asking for the data for the keyword 'enclose'.

The fifth line also asks for information that will be substituted for a keyword, but this time the keyword appears in the command file itself, and not in the master document. The prompt asks you for the name of the file you want to use as the master document. Your response will be mapped to the keyword 'filename', and when this is encountered – in the next line of the command file – 1st Mail will use the file name you have given. If in response to the final prompt you typed Pricelist, 1st Mail would look for a file called Pricelist in the same directory as the command file and process that. If the file is not in the same directory as the command file, you would need to give a full pathname or drag the file icon into the 1st Mail window.

Suppose that this is the file Pricelist:

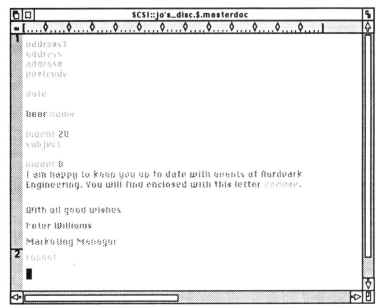

The name and address details for each letter will be retrieved from the data file Maillist. The information for the keywords date, subject and enclose has been supplied interactively in response to prompts in the 1st Mail window.

If the first entry in the data file was:

`Mr Patel,Shelford Girders Ltd,Cambridge Road,Shelford,CB2 3RT`

and you had given '17 January 1993' in response to the date prompt, 'New prices' in response to the subject prompt and 'the new 1993 price list' in response to the enclose prompt, the first letter would look like this:

Mr Patel

Shelford Girders Ltd

Cambridge Road

Shelford

CB2 3RT

17 January 1993

Dear Mr Patel

New prices

I am happy to keep you up to date with events at Aardvark Engineering. You will find enclosed with this letter the new 1993 price list.

With all good wishes

Peter Williams
Marketing Manager

Other letters would use the same information for the keywords date, subject and enclose, but would retrieve information from the data file for the other keywords.

If you had more than one data file that you used for different purposes, you could write a command file that asked for the name of the data file and the master document. This could be a general purpose command file, that filled in essential information such as the date and the subject matter that would appear in all your letters.

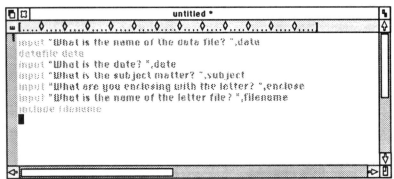

You could use a command file like this repeatedly to process each Letter and data file, but then you would have to type in the name, subject matter and enclosures each time. Instead, you could repeat the lines asking for the file names and instructing 1st Mail to use the names supplied, but not the other

INPUT lines; the values for 'date', 'subject' and 'enclosure' would then remain the same. The command file would look like this.

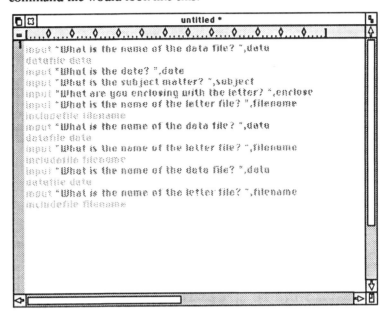

The file will use the same details for the keywords unless you use another INPUT or SETVAL command to change them. If you were processing three completely different letters, you might want only the date to be the same, so then you would have to display the prompts for the other keywords again as each letter is processed. The command file would look like this:

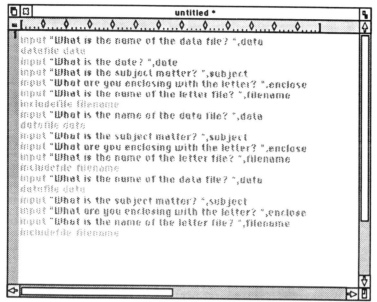

Command files are very versatile, but it takes a little practice to get used to using them and a bit of imagination to see which keywords you can usefully set interactively or with SETVAL from a command file. If you use 1st Mail a lot, it is worth persevering with command files as they can save you a lot of time.

If you have the examples disc that accompanies this book, you can try running the command files included in this chapter to see how they work. You might also be able to adapt them for your own work.

Multi-column text and labels

If you are using 1st Mail to prepare a mailshot, you will probably want it to prepare address labels to stick on the envelopes, too. You can buy address labels on a long roll, only one label wide, or you can buy single sheets or fanfold sheets with two, three or four labels across the width of the sheet. To use the first of these with 1st Mail, you just need to set a very short page length. To use the second, you need to print in two, three or four columns to use all the labels on the sheet.

Single columns of labels

If you want to print on labels, you need to treat each label as a page. This means that you need to set the page length in 1st Word Plus to the length of one label, plus the space between labels.

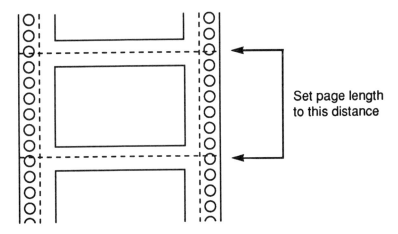

Set page length to this distance

To decide the page length and width, print some text on your labels and count the number of lines that fit between the perforations at the start of one label and at the start of the next, and across the label from left to right. Now open a 1st Word Plus document; this will be your master document. Use **Page layout** in the Layout menu to display the dialogue box that allows you to set margins and page length, and set the paper length to the number of lines you have counted. Set all the margins to zero. For example, if your label is nine lines long, you should change the settings in the dialogue box so that it looks like this:

```
┌─────────────────────────────────────────────┐
│               Page layout                     │
│                  Header                        │
│    Left    [│                            ]     │
│    Centre  [                             ]     │
│    Right   [                             ]     │
│                                                │
│                  Footer                        │
│    Left    [                             ]     │
│    Centre  [                             ]     │
│    Right   [                             ]     │
│                                                │
│ Paper length [9][↑][↓] Lines/page [9]          │
│ TOF margin  [0][↑][↓] BOF margin [0][↑][↓]     │
│ Head margin [0][↑][↓] Foot margin [0][↑][↓]    │
│                                                │
│        [ Cancel ] [   OK   ]                   │
└─────────────────────────────────────────────┘
```

You also need to set the width of the ruler so that the text fits on the label, but don't do this yet. First, add the text to your document. It will need:

◆   a read line, with all the keywords for the names and addresses of the people on your mailing list

◆   the OMITBLANK command, so that there are no blank lines left in short addresses

◆   the keywords arranged as you want the information to appear on the label

◆   a hard page break and the REPEAT command, so that 1st Mail moves to the next label before starting to print the next address.

When you have added the text, you can set the ruler to the number of characters that fit from the position you want to start printing on the label (which may not be the extreme lefthand edge) to the position where you want printing to stop. Let's assume the space you want to print in is 20 characters wide. Set the ruler width to 20 characters. You can do this by displaying the Modify ruler dialogue box (double-click on the ruler icon at the left of the ruler to call this up) and changing the length to 20:

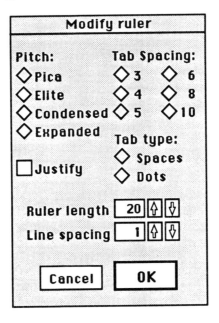

The reason for typing the text first is that if you type the READ command line after shortening the ruler, all the text won't fit on a single line, which you need it to do in order for 1st Mail to process the master document. Don't reformat the READ line after changing the ruler length. It is important that the short ruler begins right at the start of the document if you are going to print multi-column labels at any point, so don't just add a new, short ruler after the READ line.

Here is an example of a suitable master document for printing address labels. (It is on the disc that accompanies the book.)

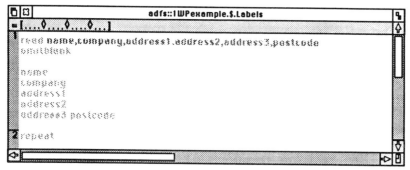

The Return before the 'name' keyword leaves a blank line at the top of the label. You can also adjust the page layout to leave a margin so that printing begins at the right vertical position on the label, if you prefer.

Using the file illustrated above with a mailing list as the data file, you will be able to print one address on each label from a continuous roll of labels. If you have sheets of labels in columns across the page, you will have to print the text in columns described below.

When you want to print the labels, drag the master document to the 1st Mail icon or window as usual. When the printer options dialogue box appears, set the Left margin offset so that printing begins on the labels and not over the perforations.

Multiple columns of labels

You need to set up the master document to print several columns of labels in just the same way as for a single column of labels, except that you need to take care to set the width of the ruler accurately. When you print multi-column text, 1st Mail calculates the gap to leave between the columns by subtracting the page width multiplied by the number of columns from the ruler length shown in the Print file dialogue box, then dividing the remainder by the number of gaps needed. For example, if you leave the setting in the Print file dialogue box at the default setting of 65, your ruler width is 20, and you want to print two columns, 1st Mail will calculate that it needs:

$65 - (20 \times 2) = 25$ spaces as the gap between the columns.

If you wanted to print three columns, the gap would be:

$$65 - \frac{(20 \times 3)}{2} = \frac{5}{2} = -2.5 \text{ spaces}$$

Depending on your printer, it may actually be able to leave a gap of a whole number of spaces only, so to get a reliable result you will need to adjust the page width and Headers/footers rule in the Print file dialogue box so that the gap comes out as a whole number of spaces.

Apart from setting the ruler width accurately, there is nothing you have to do to the master document to print multi-column labels; the other settings are made when you come to print the labels.

When you are ready to print multiple columns of labels, load a 1st Mail printer driver and drag the master document to the 1st Mail icon on the icon bar or into the 1st Mail window to display the printer options. (You can't print multiple columns to a file, because the options aren't displayed if you are printing to a file.) Use the arrow icons beside the figure for Number of columns to increase the number until it shows the number of columns of labels you want to print. An extra part of the dialogue box will appear, showing the length and text pitch of the header and footer ruler:

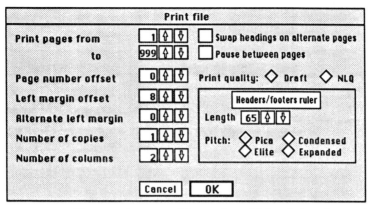

You need to set this to the width of the sheet of paper holding the labels. 1st Mail will calculate from this width and the width of the ruler you have used in the master document how wide the gaps between columns must be. It won't show you the gap it has calculated, you will just have to check the printout to see that you have set suitable values for the rulers.

Again, set the Left margin offset so that printing begins on the labels and not over the perforations.

One label will be printed at a time, beginning at the top lefthand corner of the sheet. The next to be printed will be to the right of this. The second row of labels will be printed only when the whole of the first row has been printed.

Moving on...

This is the end of the main text of the book. The appendix that follows explains how to write a printer driver to use with 1st Word Plus or 1st Mail. You will only need to do this if there is not a suitable printer driver supplied on the Acorn disc for use with your own printer.

Appendix 1: printer drivers

Why use printer drivers?

The principle of printer drivers is simple. There are 256 codes that the computer can send to the printer in the form of hexadecimal numbers. (There is a table of hexadecimal numbers in Appendix 2.) Each printer has its own way of interpreting these codes or sequences of codes, so a printer driver is needed as an interface between the computer program (1st Word Plus) and the printer. When 1st Word Plus encounters a letter, a Return or an instruction such as 'start bold text' in a document it needs to send a message to the printer in the form that the printer will understand. The printer driver acts as a translator, translating a 1st Word Plus instruction into an instruction the printer can understand. Most of the 256 possible codes are mapped directly to printing characters. There are established standards for this, and all printers share the same codes for the basic numerical and alphabetic characters. The rest of the codes are used for instructions about what the printer should do (go to the top of a page, for example, or start underlining) and for non-standard characters, such as letters used in non-English languages and characters such as # and £. There is some variation between printers on which codes they use for these instructions and characters, and the job of the printer driver is to map them correctly to the 1st Word Plus instructions. The major part of the printer driver is concerned with doing this. All you need in order to be able to create your own printer driver is a list of the codes that your printer uses for different characters and functions. You should be able to find this in the user manual for the printer.

RISC OS printer drivers

1st Word Plus and 1st Mail don't use the standard RISC OS printer drivers. However, if you have version 2.44 or later of the RISC OS printer drivers, you will be able to print text, without much highlighting and no pictures, from 1st Word Plus documents. To find out what you can expect from the version of the RISC OS printer drivers you have, open a directory display for the printer driver and select its icon. Press the middle mouse button to display the menu, and choose **Help** from the File filename submenu. A text file opens containing help information; it explains the level of support that version offers for 1st Word Plus files.

1st Word Plus printer drivers

1st Word Plus is supplied with a range of printer drivers which should suit most printers. They are mostly for daisywheel and dot-matrix printers. Although they cover the most usual makes of printer, and many printers are compatible with these, you might find either that you have difficulty deciding which printer driver is suitable for your printer or that the printer driver which is supposed to suit your printer doesn't fully work. You are then left with the problem of writing your own printer driver. You can edit any of the Acorn printer drivers, and this isn't difficult, but you need to know what to put in place of the bits that don't work. There are two stages to creating a printer driver of your own:

- editing one of the Acorn printer driver source files to suit your printer, and

- using the !1stConvrt program to convert the source code you have created into a working printer driver. (This is easy, don't be daunted by the prospect.)

Although printer drivers can seem intimidating, all you really need is patience and the manual for your printer. You'll work it out in the end.

Let's look at a printer driver to see what's involved.

The structure of a printer driver source file

Open a directory display for the 1st Word Plus Program disc, and then for the directory 1WP_Print. This contains two directories, Config and Sources. Config contains printer driver files; Sources contains the source files used to build the printer drivers. The source files are the ones you can alter; you will need to convert your new source files to configured files before you can run them. Open a directory display for Sources. Load the epson_fx printer driver source into 1st Word Plus and have a look through the text. Although we will use this one as an example, you shouldn't necessarily start with this one if you want to create your own printer driver. There is some advice later in this appendix on which printer driver source file to start with when you want to build your own printer driver.

It begins with a block of text enclosed in a box of stars. This just tells you to read about printer drivers in the 1st Word Plus manual, to edit the file using hexadecimal values for the numbers and to use !1stConvrt to make your new printer driver. Hexadecimal numbers are numbers in base 16. The table in Appendix 2 shows the corresponding hexadecimal and decimal numbers from 0 to 255. You won't need any numbers bigger than this.

The next bit of the printer driver text explains the printer name. All the lines that begin with a star (*) are comments, and have no effect on the program. The first line that doesn't have a star is the name. In this printer driver it is 'Epson FX (9-pin matrix)'. This is the name that will be displayed in the printer icon of the 1st Word Plus keypad window if you load this printer driver. You can change the name by typing over it in overstrike mode or deleting it andtyping a new name. Change the name to one you will be able to recognise easily; don't make it the same as any other of the Acorn printer drivers. The name may be up to 32 characters long. The next chunk of text is headed 'Configuration variables'. There are six variables, and these are described in the file. They are:

1 **Printer type**: Set the first figure to 1 if you have a daisywheel printer capable of micro-spacing. That means that it is capable of moving the print head by a fraction of a space to produce even-looking spacing across a line. If you have any other type of printer (such as a dot-matrix printer), set the first variable to 0.

2 **Unit width**: On a daisywheel printer, this is a measure of the width of a character. It is measured in the units that the printer itself uses, but must be expressed as a hexadecimal number. You should be able to find the width in the user manual for your printer. It might be expressed as a decimal number, in which case use the conversion chart above to find the hex equivalent and use that in the file.

If you are using a dot-matrix printer that must print each pixel twice in graphics to make the output twice as wide, set this value to 2. Otherwise, leave it at 0. If you are unsure which to use, set it to 0 first and check the printing of graphics. You can change it to 2 if the graphics look too narrow.

3 **Unit height**: You need to enter the vertical distance moved by the print head for a carriage return. Again, it must be in the printer's own units but expressed as a hexadecimal number. You should be able to find this in the printer manual.

4 **Middle of carriage position or graphics resolution**: If you have a daisywheel printer, this variable should give the position, measured in the printer's own units from the lefthand margin, at which the print head should be parked when feeding paper through the printer. The position is usually the centre of the paper. If you can't find

this information in the manual, assume that it is the centre and calculate from the carriage width where the centre position will be.

If you have a dot-matrix printer, you need to set this variable to the graphics resolution measured in pixels per inch. This value doesn't affect the printing, but is used to calculate the area shown for graphics in your document. If you set it wrongly, you won't see an accurate representation of the area covered by graphics on screen. This is inconvenient, but you'll soon see if it is wrong, and graphics will print properly anyway.

5 **Horizontal offset for bold**: If you have a daisywheel printer, set this to the offset needed for printing bold text. Again, it is measured in the printer's own units and expressed as a hexadecimal number. If you have a dot-matrix printer, set this value to 0.

6 **Pause between pages**: If you want to force the printer to pause between pages so that you can change the paper, set this to 1. Otherwise, set it to 0. You will need to set it to 1 only if you are using sheets of paper and don't have a sheet feeder attached to your printer.

When you have decided the values you need for the variables, alter the line below the descriptions of the variables so that it uses your values. The numbers must be separated by commas, as they are in the Acorn printer driver source files.

The next portion of the printer driver file sets the printer characteristics. These describe the actions your printer is capable of performing, and give the code necessary to use a procedure or give an instruction. The characteristics are numbered 0-33 (hex). You must keep these in sequence, so don't move any around; the number relates to the instruction code that 1st Word Plus uses. The description of each on the righthand side is not part of the program and is just for your information. You can't change the nature of one of the characteristics by altering its description.

Any characteristic described in a line that begins with a star is not being used. Add a star to any line that describes a characteristic your printer doesn't have or that you don't want to use (or that you don't know the control sequence for).

For each characteristic that you do want to use, the number must come at the start of the line, not preceded by a star, and it must be followed by a comma. After this, put the control code sequence needed for that function. You should be able to find these in the manual for your printer, though they may not appear in the same format as those in the Acorn printer driver file. Here are some examples:

The IBM Proprinter X24E and XL24E manual gives this information for linefeed:

```
Line Feed
    Advance the form one line.
    Syntax                   LF
    Data Structure    Hex    |0A|
                      Dec    |10|
```

From this, you need the hexadecimal code, 0A. (The 0 is actually redundant, as in 01, and you can miss it out if you like; the code is then the same as that shown in the epson_fx file, A.)

```
For carriage return, it has:

Carriage Return
```

```
Cause the data that follows to
print at left.
Syntax                CR
Data Structure        Hex      |0D|
                      Dec      |13|
```

The code you need from this is 0D, or D. Again, it is the same as the code in the Epson_fx file.

With the information from this manual, then, you could have compiled the line

1, 0D, 0A

It doesn't matter whether you include the zeros or not. The comment in the printer driver file tells you to put the carriage return code first, so you must do this.

The Epson LQ-850 and LQ-1050 manual presents the information like this:

```
CR carriage return
    format:   ASCII:          CR
              decimal:        13
              hexadecimal:    0D
              keyboard:       CTRL M
and
LF line feed
              format:         ASCII:LF
              decimal:        10
              hexadecimal:    0A
              keyboard:       CTRL H
```

The codes are the same: A for line feed and D for carriage return.

Your printer manual might not have a detailed description like this; it could have a table of codes and their meanings, like this:

ASCII codes

Decimal	Hex	Control keys	Epson FX configuration
. . .			
10	0A	CTRL J	LF
11	0B	CTRL K	VT
12	0C	CTRL M	CR

...

Here, again, line feed is 0A and carriage return is 0D. (The code in between is for vertical tab.)

These are fairly simple as the codes comprise a single hexadecimal number. For some instructions, there will be a combination of codes or characters. For example, the Canon Bubble Jet BJ300/330 manual gives the code ESC 4 to start italic print. It presents the information like this:

```
Syntax:              ESC 4

    Data Structure: hex <1B> <34>

                    dec <27> <52>
```

The hexadecimal code is given: it is the numbers that correspond to the two key presses, Escape and 4; these are 1B and 34. If you look in the epson_fx file again, you will see that the instruction for turning on italic is:

A, 1B, 34

This is the same as you would need for the Bubble Jet. The A is the instruction number (remember the list uses hex, so A is a number.) 1B corresponds to Escape, and 34 to 4. If your printer manual lists only the Escape codes, you can use the list of hexadecimal numbers and ASCII characters in the next appendix to translate the codes into hex. Don't forget to include the Escape, 1B.

Many of the characteristics and functions covered in the list in this section of the printer driver file are self-explanatory. It is obvious what 'Draft bold on' means, for example: it means begin printing bold text in draft mode (rather than NLQ, near letter quality, mode). Some of the others are less obvious, and these are explained below.

Character width: This is used for daisywheel printers only. It is likely to have three parts, the first being 1B (for Escape), and the last 81.

Forward print: Tells daisywheel printers to print from left to right; not needed with dot-matrix printers.

Backward print: Tells daisywheel printers to print from right to left; not needed with dot-matrix printers.

Vertical tab: Tells the printer to feed several lines of paper at once. It is used at the top and bottom of the page so that printing doesn't begin at the very top of the page or go to the very bottom. You don't need to use a vertical tab – the printer will use line feeds instead if necessary – and as vertical tabs can cause problems in printers that aren't as compatible with the standards as they claim to be, this option is perhaps best avoided. Put a star at the start of the line to remove it.

Horizontal tab: Tells the printer to move the print head in a smooth single movement across the paper to the start position for printing. It is not needed with daisywheel printers. The code tells the printer which character position to begin printing at.

Formfeed: Tells the printer to feed the rest of a page through and line up at the start of the next page. If this isn't defined, the printer will use linefeeds instead.

Horizontal & vertical initialisation: These are optional; they are intended to ensure that the print head is in the correct position before printing starts.

Printer reset: Resets the printer at the end of a print job; it is optional.

Form length in lines: Tells the printer how many lines there are to a page. If you use this command, it will retrieve the page length set with the Page layout dialogue box.

Set linefeed distance: Tells the printer how far to move down the page for a linefeed. This is important if graphics are to be printed correctly.

Print graphics: Tells the printer to start a line containing graphics. You can only use the coloured ink options if you are using a colour printer.

The final part of the printer driver file is a character translation table. This maps the hexadecimal codes used by your computer to the codes the printer uses to represent the characters. Again, you must keep the list in order. If there is a character which your printer does not have, leave the space after the Acorn character code blank; a space will be printed in your document if you use one of these characters. The list of characters doesn't include the standard alphabet and number set as these will be represented by the same codes.

If there are characters that you would like to be able to produce, but that are not listed in the character set for your printer, you may be able to approximate them by instructing the printer to print one character, then do a backspace, and then print another character over the top. For example, you may be able to achieve u umlaut (,) by printing a u, then doing a backspace, and then printing a double quotation mark over the top of it. To give a character code for this, you would need to use the hex codes for:

u, backspace, quotation mark

The Acorn code is FC (it's near the bottom of the file). If you looked up u, backspace and quotation mark in the character set in your printer manual and found that the codes were:

75, 88, 2C

you would need to make the line read:

FC, 75, 88, 2C

(These codes are taken from the Citizen 120-D manual.)

You might find that your printer is capable of producing characters that aren't in the standard default character set for your printer. In 1st Word Plus, these are likely to be characters that you are able to get from !1stChars but that you can't get from the keyboard without using an Alt sequence. If your printer has an alternate character set, the manual will show the characters available in it and the codes you need to use to get them. You will need to use the code to access the alternate character set, the code for the character and the code to return to the standard character set, so there will be quite a long code sequence for each character. Even if you sometimes need to use several characters from the alternate character set in succession, the printer will receive instructions for each that tell it to:

• switch to the alternate character set

• print the character you want

• return to the standard character set.

Here is an example from the NEC Pinwriter P6 plus/P7 plus User's Guide. The table of control codes and sequences includes this entry:

Code	Hex	Decimal	Function
ESC R(n)	52	82 (0-14)	Selects language character set
		(0-0E)	

This means that you have to use the sequence ESC R, followed by a number that represents the character set you want to use.

The hex code given, 52, is the code for R. Remember that you have to include the Escape, which is 1B. The code in hex will be:

1B, 52, (n)

where the n is a number that will change according to the character set you choose. You mustn't type the brackets around the n. A different page of the User's Guide shows the number you need to use for n for each character set available. Suppose you wanted to do most of your work using the UK character set, which is number 3. To set a code so that you can use the Spanish character ¿ the code sequence for the line has to:

◆   switch to the Spanish character set

◆   print ¿

◆   switch back to the English character set.

The number for the Spanish character set on the NEC Pinprinter is given as 7. This is a decimal number; remember you need to use the hex number. In this case, the hex number is the same as the decimal number. The first part of the code sequence, then, is:

`1B,52,7`

For the next part, you need to look at the table of the character set in the printer manual and find the code for ¿. This is 93 in decimal, or 5D in hex. The next part of the sequence is therefore

`5D`

The final part of the sequence must reset the English character set. The sequence is:

`1B,52,3`

The whole code sequence to print the character ø is therefore:

`1B,52,7,5D,1B,52,3`

You would need to use this code in line BF of the source file. The line would then read:

`BF, 1B, 52, 7, 5D, 1B, 52, 3  *ø - Spanish   upside down ?`

(You can include spaces to make the sequence more readable, but they are not essential).

Starting to create your own printer driver source file

If you decide that you need to create your own printer driver, either because there isn't one for your printer or because your printer is supposed to be compatible with one of the printers for which there is a printer driver, but the driver doesn't work properly with your printer, you need to choose carefully which printer driver to start with.

If you have a 9-pin dot-matrix printer and it has an Epson FX80 mode, start with the epson_fx source file.

If you have a 24-pin dot-matrix printer and it has an Epson LQ emulation mode, start with the epson_lq source file.

If you have a daisywheel printer, start with the daisy source file.

If you don't think your printer matches any of these, start with the standard printer driver.

Begin by removing the lines that refer to optional features, but that often cause problems if a printer is not fully compatible with the FX or LQ ranges. These are the vertical tab, and vertical and horizontal initialisation commands. They are in lines 4, 1F and 20 of the printer configuration section of the source file. Remove them by typing a star in front of the first number, eg:

```
*4,   1B, 42, 80,   0,   B        * Vertical tab to line
```

Begin by checking all the control code sequences for the features you want to use (such as start and stop bold printing), and putting a star in front of the features you don't want to use or can't use.

The best way to build up your printer driver is to start with minimal functionality, but a working printer driver, and then to add control sequences to build up the features you want. You can convert and test your printer driver at each stage so that if something goes wrong you know which bits you have changed and so where the error is.

Converting a source file

When you have prepared your first attempt at the printer driver, you need to save it (with a new name) in the directory Sources on your working disc. Before you can use it as a printer driver, you need to convert it. Follow these steps:

1 Open directory displays for both Config and Sources on your working disc.

2 Double-click on !1stConvrt. This doesn't load onto the icon bar, it displays the 1st Convert window, which looks like this:

Drag the icon for your edited source file to the 1st convert window and click on OK.

3 A Save dialogue box appears, showing a command file icon with the default name 1wp_print. Change the name and drag the icon into the directory display for the directory Config. This is the configured version of your new printer driver and you can now load this as a 1st Word Plus printer driver.

Once you have created your new printer driver, you need to load and test it. To load the new printer driver, display the 1st Word Plus keypad window, set the printer port and drag the icon for your new printer driver from Config onto the printer icon in the keypad window. To test it, print out the test document printtest which is in the directory 1WP_docs on the 1st Word Plus Program disc. The file includes text of different styles and pitches, and a picture to test that all aspects of your printer driver work properly. (You won't be able to print the picture if you have a daisywheel or laser printer.)

If you find that some of the special effects don't work, it is likely to be because you have used the wrong control sequences for them, or you have left a star at the front of the line for that sequence. You may not be able to get all the special features to work; it will depend on the capabilities of your printer.

When your printer driver works perfectly (or acceptably), you will probably want to make it the default printer driver so that 1st Word Plus uses this one automatically when it starts up. There is a section in chapter 15: Printing your document that explains how to change the default printer driver.

Common problems with printing

There are many things that may go wrong with printers and printer drivers and we can't cover all of them here.

If the top line of each 1st Word Plus page doesn't occur at the top line of a piece of paper, but moves up or down the page, the page length you have set with Page layout is not the same as the length of the paper you are using or the page length you have set for the printer.

If your printer claims to be Epson FX80-compatible, but it throws extra blank pages when you print with the epson_fx printer driver, add a star in front of the vertical tab line and reconfigure the source file as a new printer driver with 1stConvrt.

If you have an Epson LQ850 printer with a sheet feeder and it is throwing extra sheets of paper, add a star in front of the vertical tab line and reconfigure the source file as a new printer driver with 1stConvrt. If this doesn't work, check that the printable area of the page is set correctly. This sometimes changes when you add a sheet feeder to the printer. Print out a file of text and count the number of lines that fit on a page and check that the page length for the printer and in 1st Word Plus are set correctly.

If some of the characters you see on screen are not printed properly, the 1st Word Plus characters are not correctly mapped to the printer characters. Commonly, # and £ do not print as you expect them to. Check the code sequences the printer expects for the characters you want to print, and then correct the printer driver source file so that these are the codes given for the characters.

If graphics are not printing correctly, check the codes shown in your printer manual for all aspects of graphics printing, including:

◆ unit height (third configuration variable): set this to the line spacing in internal units. Most Epson-compatible printers print lines 12 dots apart (C in hex); the Epson LQ-800 has line spacing of 10 dots (A in hex).

◆ unit width (second configuration variable): set this to 0 or 1 initially. If you then find that you need the graphics expanded (as you may on an Atari SMM804, for example), change it to 2. This doubles the width of the printed picture by sending each pixel twice. If your picture looks squashed horizontally, try changing this. You will need to halve the graphics resolution if you set the unit width to 2.

The control sequence used to send a line containing graphics.

If nothing at all prints out, check that:

◆ the printer is turned on

◆ it is switched on-line

◆ it is connected to the computer

◆ it is connected to the port named on the 1stWord Plus keypad window (or 1st Mail printer options dialogue box)

◆ there is some paper in the printer and it isn't jammed (Avoid letting the printer run out of paper, especially if you are using 1st Mail; it can cause 1st Mail to hang.)

You may also need to check the DIP switches on your printer. These will be described in your printer manual. They control various printer settings, such as default page length. If you can make a setting in the printer driver without altering the DIP switches, it is best to do so, but don't forget that there may be some things you need to set with the DIP switches.

If multiple copies of each page are printed, this is because you have used another application (such as Acorn Desktop Publisher, for example) to print multiple copies of a document and the printer has remembered the number of copies from the last print run and is using it still. Turn off your printer and turn it on again. If this doesn't work, reset the computer as well.

Appendix 2 : Decimal and hex numbers and the Acorn character set

The following table shows decimal and hexadecimal numbers and the characters to which they are mapped in the standard Acorn Latin 1 character set (ISO 8859/1). Remember that you need to use hexadecimal codes in a printer driver source file, but decimal codes in a 1st Mail command to set characters as field or record separators or as quotation marks.

Decimal	Hexadecimal	Character code	Decimal	Hexadecimal	Character code
0	0		35	23	#
1	1		36	24	$
2	2		37	25	%
3	3		38	26	&
4	4		39	27	'
5	5		40	28	(
6	6		41	29	)
7	7		42	2A	*
8	8		43	2B	+
9	9		44	2C	,
10	A		45	2D	-
11	B		46	2E	.
12	C		47	2F	/
13	D		48	30	0
14	E		49	31	1
15	F		50	32	2
16	10		51	33	3
17	11		52	34	4
18	12		53	35	5
19	13		54	36	6
20	14		55	37	7
21	15		56	38	8
22	16		57	39	9
23	17		58	3A	:
24	18		59	3B	;
25	19		60	3C	<
26	1A		61	3D	=
27	1B		62	3E	>
28	1C		63	3F	?
29	1D		64	40	@
30	1E		65	41	A
31	1F		66	42	B
32	20	space	67	43	C
33	21	!	68	44	D
34	22	"	69	45	E

70	46	F		106	6A	j
71	47	G		107	6B	k
72	48	H		108	6C	l
73	49	I		109	6D	m
74	4A	J		110	6E	n
75	4B	K		111	6F	o
76	4C	L		112	70	p
77	4D	M		113	71	q
78	4E	N		114	72	r
79	4F	O		115	73	s
80	50	P		116	74	t
81	51	Q		117	75	u
82	52	R		118	76	v
83	53	S		119	77	w
84	54	T		120	78	x
85	55	U		121	79	y
86	56	V		122	7A	z
87	57	W		123	7B	{
88	58	X		124	7C		
89	59	Y		125	7D	}
90	5A	Z		126	7E	~
91	5B	[		127	7F	
92	5C	\		128	80	
93	5D	]		129	81	
94	5E	^		130	82	
95	5F	_		131	83	
96	60	`		132	84	
97	61	a		133	85	
98	62	b		134	86	
99	63	c		135	87	
100	54	d		136	88	
101	65	e		137	89	
102	66	f		138	8A	
103	67	g		139	8B	
104	68	h		140	8C	
105	69	i		141	8D	

142	8E		178	B2	²
143	8F		179	B3	³
144	90		180	B4	´
145	91		181	B5	µ
146	92		182	B6	¶
147	93		183	B7	·
148	94		184	B8	¸
149	95		185	B9	¹
150	96		186	BA	º
151	97		187	BB	»
152	98		188	BC	¹/₄
153	99		189	BD	¹/₂
154	9A		190	BE	³/₄
155	9B		191	BF	¿
156	9C		192	C0	À
157	9D		193	C1	Á
158	9E		194	C2	Â
159	9F		195	C3	Ã
160	A0	no-break space	196	C4	Ä
161	A1	¡	197	C5	Å
162	A2	¢	198	C6	Æ
163	A3	£	199	C7	Ç
164	A4	¤	200	C8	È
165	A5	¥	201	C9	É
166	A6	¦	202	CA	Ê
167	A7	§	203	CB	Ë
168	A8	¨	204	CC	Ì
169	A9	©	205	CD	Í
170	AA	ª	206	CE	Î
171	AB	«	207	CF	Ï
172	AC	¬	208	D0	Ð
173	AD	–	209	D1	Ñ
174	AE	®	210	D2	Ò
175	AF	—	211	D3	Ó
176	B0	°	212	D4	Ô
177	B1	±	213	D5	Õ

214	D6	Ö		250	FA	ú
215	D7	×		251	FB	û
216	D8	Ø		252	FC	ü
217	D9	Ù		253	FD	ý
218	DA	Ú		254	FE	þ
219	DB	Û		255	FF	ÿ
220	DC	Ü				
221	DD	Ý				
222	DE	Þ				
223	DF	ß				
224	E0	à				
225	E1	á				
226	E2	â				
227	E3	ã				
228	E4	ä				
229	E5	å				
230	E6	æ				
231	E7	ç				
232	E8	è				
233	E9	é				
234	EA	ê				
235	EB	ë				
236	EC	ì				
237	ED	í				
238	EE	î				
239	EF	ï				
240	F0	ð				
241	F1	ñ				
242	F2	ò				
243	F3	ó				
244	F4	ô				
245	F5	õ				
246	F6	ö				
247	F7	÷				
248	F8	ø				
249	F9	ù				

Appendix 3: Keyboard shortcuts

Ctrl-A ....Add ruler

Ctrl-B ....Find end of selection

Ctrl-C ....Cut

Ctrl-D ....Delete ruler

Ctrl-E ....End selection

Ctrl-G ....Goto page

Ctrl-K ....Clear selected text

Ctrl-L ....Show ruler

Ctrl-P ....Show ruler

Ctrl-S ....Start selection

Ctrl-T ....Find start of selection

Ctrl-U.......................Upper case

Ctrl-V ....Swap case

Ctrl-W ....Lower case

Ctrl-X ....Title word

Ctrl-Z ....Statistics

Ctrl-1....................... Add ruler

Ctrl-7.......................Goto page

F1 ....Bold

F2 ....Underline

F3 ....Italic

F4 ....Underline

F5 ....Superscript

F6 ....Subscript

F7 ....Reformat paragraph

F8 ....Delete line

F9 ....Indent

F10 ....Fixed space

F11 ....Centre text

Ctrl-F1 ....Repeat find

Ctrl-F2 ....Find

Ctrl-F3 ....Replace

Ctrl-F4 ....Add footnote

Ctrl-F5 ....Browse

Ctrl-F6 .... Add word

Ctrl-F7 ....Cut

Ctrl-F9 ....Paste

Ctrl-F10 ....Move

Ctrl-F11 ....Right-align text

Escape ....Search for misspelling

Shift left arrow   Go to start of last of current word

Shift right arrow..........Go to start of next word

Ctrl left arrow ....Go to start of line

Ctrl right arrow...........Go to end of line

Shift up arrow ....Go up a screenful of text

Shift down arrow.........Go down a screenful of text

Ctrl up arrow ....Go to start of file

Ctrl down arrow..........Go to end of file

Shift Copy..................Delete to end of word

Ctrl Copy...................Delete to end of line

Other Dabs Press Products

Dabhand Guide Books

The following are a selection of Dabhand Guides which are now available.

Also by Anne Rooney

Archimedes First Steps: A Dabhand Guide

ISBN 1-870336-73-9

240 pages

Price: £9.95

An introductory guide to the Archimedes, to guide you through those first few months of ownership. The Welcome Discs contain a wide range of useful programs which are fully documented. The book also goes further, to describe software and hardware additions to the Archimedes, how to choose and install them.

Archimedes Assembly Language: A Dabhand Guide

By Mike Ginns

ISBN 1-870336-20-8

368 pages

Book : £14.95. 3.5" disc, £9.95. Book and disc together, £21.95

Get the most from your Archimedes micro by programming directly in the machine's own language - machine code. This book covers all aspects of machine code/assembler programming for all Archimedes machines.

There is a beginner's section which takes the reader step by step through topics such as binary numbers, and logic operations.

To make the transition from BASIC to machine code as painless as possible, the book contains a section on implementing BASIC commands in machine code. All of the most useful BASIC statements are covered.

Archimedes Operating System: A Dabhand Guide

By Alex and Nick van Someren

ISBN: 1-870336-48-8

320 pages approx

Price: £14.95. 3.5in disc, £9.95. Book and disc together, £21.95

The book that is a must for every serious Archimedes owner. It describes how the Archimedes works and examines the ARTHUR operating system in microscopic detail, giving the programmer a real insight into getting the best from the Archimedes.

For the serious machine code, or BASIC, programmer included are sections on: the ARM instruction set, SWIs, graphics, Writing relocatable modules, vectors, compiled code, MEMC, VIDC, IOC and much more.

Basic V: A Dabhand Guide

By Mike Williams

ISBN 1-870336-75-5

128 pages

Price: £9.95

A practical guide to programming in BASIC V on the Acorn Archimedes. Assuming a familiarity with the BBC BASIC language in general, it describes the many new commands offered by BASIC V.

New
Budget DTP: A Dabhand Guide
by Roger Amos

ISBN 1-870336-11-9

222 pages

Price: £12.95

Every Archimedes and BBC A3000 owner receives copies of the !Draw and !Edit software, with RISC OS operating software. This book shows how these applications can be used to produce high-quality documents without the need for an expensive desktop publishing package.

A book that any impoverished but enthusiastic publisher, should not be without.

Jerry Glenwright *Acorn User May 1992*

C: A Dabhand Guide
by Mark Burgess

ISBN1-870336-16-X

512 pages

Price: £14.95

The most comprehensive introductory guide to C yet written. Gives clear and comprehensive explanations of this important programming language. Differences between various compilers are acknowledged and sections on the popular compilers for PC, and compatibles, Acorn machines including BBC and Archimedes, Atari ST and Commodore Amiga are included, with notes concerning ANSI and Kernighan and Ritchie.

AmigaDOS: A Dabhand Guide

by Mark Burgess

ISBN 1-870336-47-X

270 pages

Price: £14.95

The complete and comprehensive guide to AmigaDOS for the user of the Commodore Amiga. This book provides a unique perspective on the Amiga's powerful operating system in a way which will be welcomed by the beginner and experienced user alike. Rather than simply reiterating the Amiga manual, this book is a genuinely different approach to understanding and using the Amiga.

Simply a *must* for all Amiga owners and users!

Amiga Basic: A Dabhand Guide
by Paul Fellows

ISBN 1-870336-87-9

560 pages

Price: £15.95

A fully structured tutorial to using AmigaBASIC on the whole range of Commodore Amiga computers.

WordStar 1512: A Dabhand Guide
Including WordStar Express

by Bruce Smith

ISBN 1-870336-17-8

240 pages

Book: £12.95. Disc: 5.25in, £7.95; book and disc together, £17.95

A comprehensive tutorial and reference guide to WordStar 1512 and WordStar Express.

VIEW: A Dabhand Guide

by Bruce Smith

ISBN 1-870336-00-3

248 pages

Book: £12.95. Disc: DFS 5.25in, £7.95 ADFS; 3.5in, £9.95. Book and disc together, £17.95 (ADFS £19.95)

The most comprehensive tutorial and reference guide written about using the VIEW wordprocessor.

Mini Office II: A Dabhand Guide

By Bruce Smith & Robin Burton

ISBN 1-870336-55-0

256 pages

Price: £9.95

Official tutorial and reference guide to the award winning Mini Office II software. Covers everyday use of all modules.

Master Operating System: A Dabhand Guide

by David Atherton

ISBN 1-870336-01-1

272 pages

Book: £12.95. Disc: DFS 5.25in, £7.95 ADFS; 3.5in, £9.95. Book and disc together, £17.95 (ADFS £19.95)

The definitive reference work for programmers of the BBC Model B+, Master 128 and Master Compact computers.

SuperCalc 3: A Dabhand Guide
by Dr. A. A. Berk

ISBN 1-870336-65-8

240 pages

Price: £14.95

A complete tutorial and reference guide for one of the most popular pieces of software of all time - SuperCalc spreadsheet for the Amstrad PC1512, 1640 and other PC-compatibles.

Master 512 Technical Guide: A Dabhand Guide
by Robin Burton

ISBN 1-870336-80-1

417 pages

Price: £14.95

The definitive hardware and software reference for the dedicated users of the Master 512, Acorn's PC-compatible upgrade for BBC and Master computers.

Master 512 User Guide: A Dabhand Guide
by Chris Snee

ISBN 1-870336-14-3

224 pages

Book: £14.95 Disc £7.95. Book and disc £19.95 (£21.95 3.5")

The most significant tutorial and reference guide for the Master 512.

Windows, A User's Guide: A Dabhand Guide

By Ian Sinclair

ISBN 1-870336-63-1

396 pages

Price: £14.95

A comprehensive guide to Microsoft Windows™ for the IBM PC and compatibles.

Psion LZ, A User's Guide to OPL: A Dabhand Guide

By Ian Sinclair

ISBN 1-870336-92-5

224 pages

Price: £12.95

Enjoy better understanding and complete command of your Psion LZ with this guide.

Z88: A Dabhand Guide

By Trinity Concepts

ISBN 1-870336-60-7

296 pages

Price £14.95

An indispensable guide for all users of the Z88 portable computer.

Z88 Pipedream: A Dabhand Guide

By John Allen

ISBN 1-870336-61-5

240 pages

Price: £14.95

A definitive guide to PipeDream, the revolutionary integrated business software package on the Cambridge Computer Z88 portable computer.

Forthcoming Books for 1992

The Amstrad PCW Series: A Dabhand Guide
By John Atherton ISBN 1-870336-50-X.

Ability Plus: A Dabhand Guide
by Geoff Cox ISBN 1-870336-51-8

Wordstar 6: A Dabhand Guide
By Geoff Cox ISBN 1-870336-88-7

Basic on the PC: A Dabhand Guide
By Geoff Cox ISBN 1-870336-96-8

Windows 3.1: A Dabhand Guide
By Jon Mountfort ISBN 1-870336-66-6

Impression: A Dabhand Guide
By Anne Rooney ISBN 1-870336-10-0

Basic Wimp Programming: A Dabhand Guide
By Alan Senior ISBN 1-870336-53-4

Psion Series 3: A Dabhand Guide
By Patrick Hall ISBN 1-870336-97-6

Please note:

All future publications are in an advanced state of preparation. We reserve the right to alter and adapt them without notification. If you would like more information about Dabs Press, books and software, then drop us a line at 22 Warwick Street, Prestwich, M25 7HN.

Index

Q

quotation marks in data files 186-187, 189
QUOTES 189
Qume printer drivers 133-134

R

RAGGED 178
READ 174-175, 185
record 184-186
record separator 188
RECORDSEP 188
Reformat 49-50
removing page break 75-76
removing rulers 57-58
removing tabs 55
removing words from the dictionary 105-106
renaming printer driver 137-139
REPEAT 175-176
Replace 62-64, 90
Return 33-35
right-aligned text 48, 50-51
RISC OS printer drivers 135-136, 143, 148-149, 222
RS423 interface 131
ruler 25, 48, 52-58, 80
ruler length 53-54
!Run file 146-149

S

saving ASCII text 123-125
saving documents 121-122, 124-125
saving selections 122-123, 124-125
saving supplementary dictionary 99-100
screen mode 155
scroll bars 25
search see Findselecting text 41-43
serial port 130-131
Set mark 68

There is a disc to accompany this book, to obtain this disc please fill in the order form below.

DABS PRESS Order Form

1st Word Plus disc

£7.95 inc. VAT

Please send me the accompanying disc to Mastering 1st Word Plus: A Dabhand Guide.

I enclose a cheque/official order Number:

....

or My Access/Visa No. is

☐☐☐☐ ☐☐☐☐ ☐☐☐☐ ☐☐☐☐

Expires ☐☐ ☐☐

Price includes VAT and postage in the UK. Foreign readers, please pay the same amount as there is no VAT, but additional postage costs.

Name ....

Address..

....

....

....